The crew of the <u>Endurance</u>

Top row: Holness and Bakewell. Second row: McNish, James, Wild, Worsley, Stephenson (above Worsley), Hudson, How, Green. Third row: Cheetham, Crean, Hussey, Greenstreet, Shackleton, Sir Daniel Gooch (who sailed as far as South Georgia as a "dog minder"), Rickinson, Hurley. Front row: Clark, Wordie, Macklin, Marston, McIlroy.

Also by Caroline Alexander

One Dry Season
The Way to Xanadu
Battle's End
Mrs. Chippy's Last Expedition

The Endurance

Cutting through the pack ice

THE
Endurance

Shackleton's
Legendary Antarctic
Expedition

Caroline Alexander

BLOOMSBURY

First published in Great Britain 1998
This paperback edition published 1999
Bloomsbury Publishing Plc, 38 Soho Square, London W1V 5DF
Copyright © 1998 by Caroline Alexander
The moral right of the author has been asserted.
A CIP catalogue record for this book is available from the British Library

ISBN 0 7475 4670 3
10 9 8 7 6 5 4

Grateful acknowledgment is made to Sheil Land Associates Ltd., London, for permission to reprint excerpts from *The Endurance* by Frank Arthur Worsley, copyright © 1931 by F. A. Worsley.

Printed & bound in Great Britain by Butler & Tanner
First Edition
In Association with the American Museum of Natural History

Photographs on the following pages are reproduced with the permission of the picture library of the Royal Geographical Society, London: opening, half title, frontispiece, epigraph, 2, 13, 14, 17, 20, 24, 25, 26, 27, 28, 29, 30, 31, 32, 33, 34, 35, 36, 37, 40, 41, 43, 45 (both), 46, 47, 48, 50, 51 (both), 52 (top), 54, 55 (both), 58, 61, 63, 67, 68, 69, 70, 72, 73, 74, 75, 77, 78 (both), 79, 80, 81, 83, 84, 85, 86, 87, 90, 91, 92, 94, 96, 97, 98, 100 (both), 101, 102, 103, 105, 106, 109, 110, 111, 112, 113, 115, 120, 128, 129, 130, 131, 132, 133, 134 (right), 135, 136, 137 (both), 138, 139, 140, 141, 142, 163, 170, 172, 173, 174, 175, 177, 180, 183, 184, 186, 191, 203, 210. Photographs copyright © 1998 by the Royal Geographical Society.

Photographs on the following pages are reproduced with the permission of the picture library of the Scott Polar Research Institute, Cambridge, England: dedication, second half title, 11, 12 (both), 16, 18, 19, 22, 23, 42, 44, 52 (bottom), 53, 57, 59 (all), 60, 62, 64 (both), 65, 66, 76, 82, 99, 114, 134 (left), 154, 201, 204.

Photograph on page 135 is reproduced with the permission of the Mitchell Library, State Library of New South Wales, Sydney, Australia.

TO MRS. CHIPPY

Who pioneered the way

Blackborow with Mrs. Chippy

Never for me the lowered banner,
never the last endeavour.

—SIR ERNEST SHACKLETON

The Rescue

The Endurance

Sir Ernest Shackleton

The Heroic Age

The captain of the ship, Frank Worsley, would remember the day vividly ever afterward. It was July, midwinter in Antarctica, and the darkness of the long polar night had been upon them for many weeks. The temperature was −30° Fahrenheit, and around the ship, extending to the horizon in all directions, was a sea of ice, white and mysterious under the clear, hard stars. From time to time, the shriek of the wind outside broke all conversation. Away in the distance, the ice would groan, and Worsley and his two companions would listen to its ominous voice as it travelled to them across the frozen miles. Sometimes, the little ship would quiver and groan in response, her wooden timbers straining as the pressure from millions of tons of ice, set in motion by some faraway disturbance, at last reached her resting place and nipped at her resilient sides. One of the three men spoke.

"She's pretty near her end. . . . The ship can't live in this, Skipper. You had better make up your mind that it is only a matter of time. It may be a few months, and it may be only a question of weeks, or even days . . . but what the ice gets, the ice keeps."

The year was 1915. The speaker was Sir Ernest Shackleton, one of the most renowned polar explorers of his day, and the third man was Frank Wild, his second-in-command. Their ship, *Endurance*, was trapped at latitude 74° south, deep in the frozen waters of Antarctica's Weddell Sea. Shackleton had been intent on an ambitious mission: He and his men had travelled to the south to claim one of the last remaining prizes in exploration, the crossing on foot of the Antarctic continent.

Since December 1914, the *Endurance* had battled unusually heavy ice conditions, travelling more than 1,000 miles from the remote whaling stations on the island of South Georgia, at the gateway to the Antarctic Circle. One hundred miles short of

Frank Hurley
The expedition's gifted and gritty photographer poses for a studio shot in his Burberry helmet and tunic.

3

her intended harbor, new ice conditions brought the *Endurance* to a halt. A northeast gale blowing on and off for six straight days compressed the pack against the Antarctic ice shelf, trapping the ship fast within it. Days later, the temperature plummeted to 9°, as good as cementing the loose pack for the winter. Meanwhile, the leisurely, unrelenting northerly drift of the Weddell Sea carried the *Endurance* within the pack farther and farther from the land it had come so close to reaching.

When Shackleton embarked upon his Imperial Trans-Antarctic Expedition, he was already a national hero with two polar expeditions behind him, including one that had taken him to within 100 miles of the South Pole, the farthest south anyone had travelled at that time. Yet for all the heroism of these earlier efforts, neither had accomplished what it had set out to do. By the time Shackleton headed south again in 1914, the prize of the South Pole, which he had twice sought, had been claimed by others. Undaunted, he had turned his sights upon a last great venture—the crossing of the Antarctic continent from the Weddell to the Ross Sea. The preparations for the *Endurance* expedition had been all-consuming; not the least of Shackleton's tasks had been raising the funds to make it possible. He was forty years of age, and he had summoned all his experience as explorer and organizer to bear on this ambitious undertaking. Shackleton could not yet know it, but the trans-Antarctic expedition would amount to another unsuccessful venture. Yet ultimately it would be for this, the failed *Endurance* expedition, that he would be most remembered.

Antarctic exploration of the early twentieth century was unlike exploration of anywhere else on earth. No dangerous beasts or savage natives barred the pioneering explorer's way. Here, with wind speeds up to nearly 200 miles an hour and temperatures as extreme as −100° Fahrenheit, the essential competitions were pure and uncomplicated, being between man and the unfettered force of raw Nature, and man and the limits of his own endurance. Antarctica was also unique in being a place that was genuinely discovered by its explorers. No indigenous peoples had been living there all along, and the men who set foot on the continent during this age could authentically claim to have been where no member of humankind had ever cast a shadow.

Beginning in 1914 and ending in 1917, straddling the First World War, the *Endurance* expedition is often said to have been the last in the Heroic Age of polar exploration. The significance and ambition of Shackleton's proposed trans-Antarctic crossing is best appreciated within a context of the ordeals of heroism—and egotism—that had played out before. Indeed, Shackleton's greatness as a leader on the *Endurance* owes much to the sometimes insane suffering of his earlier Antarctic experiences.

The Heroic Age began when the ship *Discovery*, under the command of Captain Robert Falcon Scott, set out for Antarctica's McMurdo Sound in August 1901. Despite public talk of scientific advancement, the real objective of this first inland expedition, as of subsequent ones, was to reach the as yet unclaimed South Pole and win it for Britain. Scott chose two men to accompany him on this first bid for the pole—Dr. Edward Wilson, a physician, zoologist, and close friend; and Lieutenant Ernest Shackleton, a twenty-eight-year-old merchant service officer, whose commissions had taken him to Africa and the East. On November 2, the three men set out with nineteen sledging dogs and five loaded sledges. They faced an unspeakably daunting challenge, a round-trip journey of more than 1,600 miles, hard sledging all the way, through an entirely unknown and uncharted environment.

By day, the three man-hauled their loads with or without the aid of the dogs, ferrying their supplies in time-consuming relays. By night they meticulously divided their meager food into three equal portions and read Darwin to one another before retiring to their frozen sleeping bags. They starved, they suffered from scurvy. The dogs sickened and dropped, and were butchered to feed the survivors. Scott pushed his band on to 82°17′ south, 745 miles north of the pole, before acknowledging their desperate situation and reluctantly giving the order to turn back. By this time, Shackleton was spitting blood, undone by scurvy, and sometimes had to be carried on the sledge. On February 3, 1903, three months after setting out, they arrived back at their ship. The last leg of this terrible journey had been a race for their very lives.

This first Antarctic trek established the pattern of heroic suffering that would characterize subsequent British expeditions. Yet even a casual perusal of the explorers' diaries suggests this suffering was unnecessary. Less than three weeks into their journey Wilson notes: "Dogs getting very tired and very slow (19 November). . . . The dogs made terribly heavy weather of it today, and the dog driving has become the most exasperating work (21 November). . . . Dogs very weary indeed and terribly slack and the driving of them has become a perfectly beastly business (24 November)." Day after day, one follows the downward spiral of these wretched, exhausted animals. It is unpleasant reading.

Scott's own diary sounds more alarms: "On the whole our ski so far have been of little value. . . . [T]he dogs, which have now become only a hindrance, were hitched on behind the sledges," Scott wrote on January 6, 1903. The following day he notes that they "dropped all the dogs out of the traces and pulled steadily ourselves for seven hours, covering ten good miles by sledge-meter. . . . [T]he animals walked pretty steadily alongside the sledges." It is a stunningly improbable image: Three men walking across Antarctica at about a mile an hour with their skis securely strapped to the sledges, accompanied by a pack of dogs. Scott and his companions had not taken the time to become proficient on skis, nor did they have any knowl-edge of driving dogs. Their prodigious difficulties, therefore, were the result of almost inconceivable incompetence, not necessity. And the men were starving—not because unforeseen disaster had taken their supplies, but because they had not rationed sufficient food. Shackleton, the biggest of the men, suffered the most because he required more fuel than did the others.

And they had quarrelled. Scott and Shackleton could not have been temperamen-tally more dissimilar and had virtually no rapport. As a product of the navy, Scott established a rigid order predicated upon rank and rules; on the *Discovery*, in the middle of the Antarctic, he put a man in irons for disobedience. Shackleton, an Anglo-Irishman from the ranks of the merchant marine, was charismatic, mixing eas-ily with both crew and officers. He had been chosen to accompany Scott on account of his physical strength. The long days of white silence, the unrelenting tedium and hardship, the unrelieved close quarters—all these factors must have shredded the men's nerves. Wilson appears to have been forced to act as peacemaker on more than one occasion. Years later, Scott's second-in-command told the story that after break-fast one day Scott had called to the other men, "Come here, you bloody fools." Wil-son asked if he was speaking to him, and Scott replied no. "Then it must have been me," said Shackleton. "Right, you're the worst bloody fool of the lot, and every time you dare to speak to me like that, you'll get it back." It is a surreal encounter, a piece of absurd theater—three men alone at the ends of the earth in a virtual whiteout, hissing at one another.

On their return to the *Discovery*, Scott invalided Shackleton home. Though morti-fied by his early return to England, Shackleton arrived home as a hero who had gone farther south than anyone before. And as the lone available authority on the expedi-tion, he received more attention than would otherwise have been the case. This recognition, he must have known, would prove valuable should he one day wish to stage his own expedition. In any case, he would never again submit to the leadership of another man.

The son of a physician, Shackleton was comfortably middle-class. Born in County Kildare, Ireland, he had lived briefly in Dublin as a child, before his parents moved their family permanently to England. He was the eldest of two sons and had eight doting sisters. Shackleton had been educated at Dulwich College, a middle-class pub-lic school of high reputation, before joining the British Merchant Navy at age six-teen. Prior to volunteering for the National Antarctic Expedition, under Captain Scott, he had been a third officer with a prestigious merchant service line. Charming and handsome, with dark, brooding looks, Shackleton was a man of romantic ambi-tions, and in later life would fall under the spell of many a fruitless fortune-making scheme. Polar exploration appealed to both his poetical nature and his urgent aspiration to secure a position in the class-riven world of his time. The *Discovery* expedition had opened the door onto a more glamorous and congenial life; it was a way out of the middle class.

In 1904, Shackleton married his patient sweetheart, Emily Dorman, who, as the daughter of a well-to-do lawyer, was of modestly independent means. Now more than ever, he wanted to establish a name for himself. When ventures into journalism, business, and even politics failed, Shackleton moved towards his ultimate destiny. In early 1907, he obtained seed money for a new expedition to the South Pole. In August of the same year, after less than seven months of frantic organization, his ship *Nimrod* set sail for the south.

Shackleton had learned much on the *Discovery* expedition, but he had not learned all he should; the *Nimrod* departed with ten Manchurian ponies and only nine dogs—even though expeditions to the Arctic had by this time proved that dog teams were the only practical mode of polar transportation. Shackleton had also made little progress in learning how to ski, and much of his mountaineering equipment would prove inadequate.

These shortcomings notwithstanding, on October 29, 1908, Shackleton departed from his base at Cape Royds over the Great Ice Barrier on his second journey south with three companions and a team of four ponies. Once again, the pattern of man-hauling and suffering began. The ponies slipped and floundered, at times sinking up to their bellies in the snow. Eventually, most would be shot and eaten. By early December, Shackleton and his three companions—Frank Wild, Dr. Eric Marshall, and Lieutenant Jameson Adams—had reached the tongue of a massive, hitherto unknown glacier that flowed from the range of mountains abutting the Great Ice Barrier. Christened by Shackleton the Beardmore Glacier after one of the expedition's patrons, it was to be his party's gateway from the ice shelf on which they had been travelling to the continental plateau behind the mountains. It provided a fearful, glittering passage. Without crampons the men, accompanied by Socks, the lone remaining and unshod pony, fought their way up the dangerous tongue of ice. On the third day, the pony fell down a crevasse to his death. Suffering from snow-blindness, hunger, and frostbite, the men struggled beyond the Beardmore on to 88°23′ south—approximately 100 miles short of the pole. Here, Shackleton took realistic stock of their meager provisions and failing strength, and made the bitter decision to turn back while survival was still possible. Near journey's end, with Adams critically ailing, Shackleton and Frank Wild dumped all the gear they could spare so as to make a desperate dash for the relief of their companion. They travelled thirty-six hours with little rest, only to find that the base camp they had so long dreamed of was deserted. They were discovered shortly afterward when the *Nimrod* returned with a search party preparing to winter over and look for their bodies.

Shackleton's effort surpassed Scott's southern record by some 360 miles. Although he and his companions had suffered greatly, they survived and, thanks in great part to the fresh pony meat, had kept scurvy at bay. Back in England, Shackleton became a national hero and was knighted. Although he publicly made tentative plans for another southern expedition, this one to explore the land west of Cape Adare in the Ross Sea, his time was consumed by efforts to pay off the *Nimrod*'s debts. For the next couple of years, Shackleton hit the lecture trail, dictated a best-selling book called *The Heart of the Antarctic*, and even turned the *Nimrod* into a museum, to which he charged admission. Meanwhile Scott, with the prayers and good wishes of the nation, headed back for another assault on the South Pole. Shackleton, mired in financial obligations, could only read the headlines and wait.

Scott's last journey is, of course, an epic of its own. In October 1910, the news broke that the Norwegian explorer Roald Amundsen had secretly turned back from a projected trip to the Arctic and was headed south, intent on beating the British to the pole. The race was on. Both expeditions set out in October 1911, Scott from Cape Evans, near his old base, Amundsen from the Bay of Whales, some distance to the east. Scott's party, bogged down by a bewildering array of modes of transportation—ponies, such as Shackleton had already proved to be useless, motor sledges that didn't work, and dogs that no one knew how to drive—slogged their way south, adhering closely to Shackleton's route and playing out the now traditional drama of starvation and hardship. Amundsen and his four companions, travelling by ski with a team of fifty-two superbly conditioned and trained dogs, averaged a comfortable fifteen to twenty miles a day in comparison with Scott's ragged ten- to thirteen-mile daily pace. On their homeward run, the Norwegians covered up to thirty miles a day.

"Cannot understand what the English mean when they say that dogs cannot be used here," Amundsen puzzled in his diary. On January 16, 1912, Scott and his debilitated team staggered to 89° south to find the snow crisscrossed with the tracks of Amundsen's party.

"The worst has happened," Scott allowed in his diary. "All the day dreams must go." The following day, the dispirited party continued to the pole, planted their flag, took their notes and photographs, and prepared to turn back.

"Great God! this is an awful place," wrote Scott. "Now for the run home and a desperate struggle. I wonder if we can do it."

They could not. Each of the five men in Scott's company died on the ice. The end came in a raging blizzard that trapped the party, down to three survivors, in their single tent, a mere eleven miles south of a vital supply depot. Now Scott unfurled his real greatness—not for expeditionary leadership, but for language.

"We shall die like gentlemen," he wrote to the expedition's treasurer in England. "I think this will show that the Spirit of pluck and power to endure has not passed out of our race." His Message to the Public is a litany of excuses stirringly presented—failed pony transport, weather, snow, "frightfully rough ice," "a shortage of fuel in our depots for which I cannot account," the illness of his brave companion Titus Oates. Yet, it is a cynical reader indeed who remains unmoved by this tide of final words penned in the gallant little tent and poured forth into the white night that raged around it.

"Had we lived, I should have had a tale to tell of hardihood, endurance, and courage of my companions, which would have stirred the heart of every Englishman. These rough notes and our dead bodies must tell the tale."

"It seems a pity," he wrote as his diary's last entry, on March 29, "but I do not think I can write more."

It took nearly a year for Scott's last words to reach the outside world. When they did, in February 1913, they plunged the entire empire into deep mourning. "With the sole exception of the death of Nelson in the hour of victory, there has been nothing so dramatic," a journalist noted. Scott's tragedy was commemorated in the press and in the pulpit. In the public telling, his party's fatal, perverse blunders were not merely forgotten but evaporated out of existence. A myth was born, and propagated by the eventual publication of Scott's diaries, subtly edited by Sir James Barrie, the author of *Peter Pan* and a master of sentimental prose.

This, then, was the background against which Shackleton pulled together his Imperial Trans-Antarctic Expedition. Setting out the year after the news of Scott's death, the *Endurance* expedition was ambivalently perceived as both a gripping national event and an anticlimax. In the public imagination, Antarctica was very much the place for heroic adventure; yet it seemed unthinkable that any future success could surpass Scott's glorious failure.

Shackleton's aims, as stated in his expedition's prospectus, were compelling:

From the sentimental point of view, it is the last great Polar journey that can be made. It will be a greater journey than the journey to the Pole and back, and I feel it is up to the British nation to accomplish this, for we have been beaten at the conquest of the North Pole and beaten at the conquest of the South Pole. There now remains the largest and most striking of all journeys—the crossing of the Continent.

Shackleton eventually cobbled together funds for his grand venture. His principal backers were the British government and Sir James Key Caird, a wealthy Scottish jute manufacturer who contributed a princely gift of £24,000. Other benefactors of note were Miss Janet Stancomb-Wills, daughter of a tobacco tycoon, and Dudley Docker, of the Birmingham Small Arms Company. Lesser outright gifts came from the Royal Geographical Society, other individuals, and public schools throughout England, who underwrote the dog-sledging teams.

Another source of money was the advance sale of all "news and pictorial rights" to the expedition. Antarctica was the first continent to be discovered by camera. Beginning with Scott's first expedition in 1902, photography had captured the slow inroads made on its white, inviolate vastness. These photographic records had proved to be not only of historic and geographic interest, but also highly popular. Herbert Ponting's *90° South*, a cinematographic tribute to Scott's last expedition, was still a favorite when Shackleton's party set out. Mindful of this, Shackleton formed the Imperial Trans Antarctic Film Syndicate specifically to exploit all film rights to the expedition, exclusive story rights having been sold to the *Daily Chronicle*.

Shackleton purchased a ship from Norway's famous Framnaes shipyard, long a supplier of polar vessels. A 300-ton wooden barquentine, she was named *Polaris* and had never sailed. She was 144 feet long, built of planks of oak and Norwegian fir up to two and one-half feet thick, and sheathed in greenheart, a wood so tough it cannot be worked by conventional means. Every detail of her construction had been scrupulously, even lovingly, planned by a master shipwright to ensure her maximum strength. She was, it seemed, ideally equipped to withstand the ice. Shackleton renamed her *Endurance* after his family motto: *Fortitudine Vincimus*—"by endurance we conquer."

In fact two vessels were required. While Shackleton intended to commence his overland trek from the Weddell Sea, his plans called for a relief ship to sail to his old base at Cape Royds in the Ross Sea. From there, a six-man depot-laying party would advance inland, depositing caches of supplies for the use of Shackleton's transcontinental party when it slogged its way overland from the other side. For this task, Shackleton purchased the *Aurora*, an old-time sealer built in 1876 that had served a former colleague, the great Australian explorer Douglas Mawson.

By August, all seemed ready. Although the British press had shown keen interest in Shackleton's latest polar adventure, the departure of the *Endurance* from its London dock on August 1, 1914, was eclipsed by more important news: Germany had declared war on Russia, and a European war was now imminent. Having sailed from London to Plymouth, the ship was still in British waters when the order for general mobilization was given on Monday, August 4. After consulting with his crew, Shack-

leton placed the *Endurance* and her company at the disposal of the government, believing "there were enough trained and experienced men among us to man a destroyer." Privately, he must have held his breath: After so much work and planning, to be thwarted at the start! But the one-word telegraphed reply from the Admiralty dissolved his fears: "Proceed." A longer cable from Winston Churchill, First Lord of the Admiralty, followed, saying that the authorities desired the expedition to take place, and on August 8, the *Endurance* set sail from Plymouth.

With the example of Amundsen's triumph of efficiency vividly before him, Shackleton had taken what were by British standards enormous pains with his preparations. He had succeeded in having seconded to the expedition a young officer from the Royal Marines who, although officially the motor expert, was also proficient enough on skis to act as an instructor for the company. The *Illustrated London News* ran a photograph of Shackleton testing his new domed tents in Norway. He had consulted with professional nutritionists regarding sledging rations and, heeding the adamant advice of the Norwegians, arranged to have sixty-nine Canadian sledge dogs delivered to Buenos Aires, where the *Endurance* would pick them up on her way south. These were, according to his second-in-command, "a mixture of wolf & about any kind of big dog, Collie, Mastiff, Great Dane, Bloodhound, Newfoundland, Retriever, Airedale, Boarhound etc."

Despite these efforts his party was not as shipshape as Shackleton may have thought. He had his dogs, but his sole experienced dog trainer and driver, a Cana-

Owd Bob

The sledging dogs were not huskies, but a mixed collection of big dogs who had shown in Canada that they were adapted to the cold. "Actually there is not one that is not to some extent a mongrel."
(Lees, diary)

Soldier

Wild's team leader

dian, dropped out at the last minute when Shackleton was unwilling to pay a hefty insurance deposit; also left behind were worm pills, which, as matters turned out, the dogs would desperately need. Shackleton's plans for the continental crossing called for an average of fifteen miles' sledging a day, very close to Amundsen's outward-going average of sixteen—and yet only one of Shackleton's men left England actually knowing how to ski.

But the expedition had intangible assets deriving from Shackleton's previous endeavors. In 1909, having trudged to 88° south, 100 miles short of the pole, he had turned his back on certain glory and led his men on the long journey home. After so many hard miles, it was excruciating to leave the unclaimed prize for another man—let alone a rival. Yet Shackleton resisted persuading himself that he could safely cover those forgone miles, or that they counted for more than life itself. Had he been less self-possessed, or more desperate for glory, undoubtedly Ernest Shackleton would have been the first man to stand at the South Pole—and he and his trusting men would have died somewhere close to where Scott and his party perished in their little tent. Shackleton's decision to turn back was more than a singular act of courage; it bespoke the dogged optimism that was the cornerstone of his character. Life would always offer more chances.

"One has the feeling that if it had been Shackleton who lost to Amundsen at the pole, he would have met up with the Norwegians on the way back, and they would have all held a big celebratory party," a distinguished polar historian once told me.

The despondency that clearly crushed Scott on his loss to Amundsen was unknown to Shackleton. He seems to have been possessed of a ferocious but handily adaptable single-mindedness: Once intent on achieving the pole, he strained every nerve to get there; but when survival became the challenge, he was not distracted by such demons as regret or the fear of being perceived a failure.

Early in his career, Shackleton became known as a leader who put his men first. This inspired unshakable confidence in his decisions, as well as tenacious loyalty. During the march back from 88° south, one of Shackleton's three companions, Frank Wild, who had not begun the expedition as a great admirer of Shackleton, recorded in his diary an incident that changed his mind forever. Following an inadequate meal of pemmican and pony meat on the night of January 31, 1909, Shackleton had privately forced upon Wild one of his own biscuits from the four that he, like the others, was rationed daily.

"I do not suppose that anyone else in the world can thoroughly realize how much generosity and sympathy was shown by this," Wild wrote, underlining his words. "I DO by GOD I shall never forget it. Thousands of pounds would not have bought that one biscuit."

When Shackleton headed south on the *Endurance* in August 1914, it was with Frank Wild as his second-in-command. Wild never forgot the private act of kindness, and his adamantine loyalty to Shackleton would prove to be one of the expedition's major assets. However deficient the preparations for the Imperial Trans-Antarctic Expedition may have been, on one point it was secure: Its men had a leader who had shown signs of greatness. To be sure, Shackleton would fail once more to achieve his expedition's goal; in fact, he was destined never to set foot on the Antarctic continent again. Nevertheless, he would see his men through one of the greatest epics of survival in the annals of exploration.

Frank Wild

Shackleton's loyal second-in-command, according to Macklin, was "always calm, cool or collected, in open lanes or in tight corners he was just the same; but when he did tell a man to jump, that man jumped pretty quick."

On the bow of the <u>Endurance</u>, December 9, 1914

"Misty weather obscuring distant view & at 4:15 run into the pack again." (Hurley, diary)

South

Leaving England on August 8, 1914, the *Endurance* headed south by way of Madeira, Montevideo, and Buenos Aires, where it spent nearly two weeks loading stores while adjustments were made to the crew. Shackleton himself did not join the expedition until it reached Buenos Aires in mid-October. All had not been easy on this first leg south. Short of fuel, the *Endurance* had burned the wood allocated for the magnetician's Antarctic hut, and under the command of the high-spirited Captain Frank Worsley, a New Zealander, discipline aboard ship had been markedly lax. Worsley himself mentions an altercation in Madeira, noting with some gusto, "Irving was cut with a sword on top of his head & Barr had had a large flower pot broken in his face." Significantly, shortly after Shackleton met his ship, the names Irving and Barr, along with two others now forgotten, disappear from the ship's roll.

Also joining the *Endurance* in Buenos Aires, a few days before Shackleton, was James Francis Hurley, a gifted Australian photographer, and the man upon whom Shackleton's film syndicate had pinned its hopes. Hurley was born for this kind of venture. Independent and stubborn even as a boy, he ran away from home at the age of thirteen, finding work with the local ironworks, which in turn took him to the Sydney dockyards. While a teenager he bought his first camera, a 15-shilling Kodak box paid for with a shilling a week. Hurley's first professional work was taking pictures for postcards, but he had quickly moved on to more congenial assignments.

On October 26, the *Endurance*, painted black and loaded with fresh supplies as well as sixty-nine Canadian sledging dogs, set sail for the South Atlantic. The company had not been particularly reassured to learn that the unusually wet weather in Buenos Aires indicated that the ice had not broken in the Weddell Sea. Nor could the state of the funding, shaky as usual, have contributed to Shackleton's peace of mind. James Wordie, the expedition's geologist, had advanced personal monies to Shackle-

ton for the purchase of fuel. And although the ship carried a wireless receiver, the expedition could not afford to purchase a transmitting plant. Nevertheless, the *Endurance* was bound at last for South Georgia, east of the Falklands, her final port of call.

Like most expeditions of this kind, the ship carried a mixed company of officers and scientists, as well as seamen. In Scott's expeditions, the two groups had been strictly segregated in naval fashion, but under Shackleton less attention was paid to niceties of class.

"So I find we have got to work!" wrote marine captain Thomas Orde-Lees in his diary. "The crew of the ship is insufficient for her needs as a sailing ship & so whenever she is under sail & a sail requires altering in any way we—the scientists, six of us—have to pull on the ropes. . . . Rope pulling makes the hands sore & the ropes are exceedingly dirty & tarry but it is good exercise."

Lees was Shackleton's ski expert, and was also in charge of the aero-propellered motor sledges that were destined not to work. His diary, the most chatty and opinionated of those kept by expedition members, is also one of the most informative. Lees was a public-school man, educated at Marlborough. No one found the menial tasks more distasteful, and yet even he could discern their purpose.

"One can always have a bath afterwards, & I suppose it is good for one from a disciplinary point of view," he conceded in his diary. Just how vital this discipline would prove to the well-being of the company as a whole not even Shackleton could have known.

The *Endurance* arrived at South Georgia on November 5, eleven days after leaving Buenos Aires, in a mist of snow squalls that obscured a jagged, precipitous coastline. The company were greeted warmly by the island's small population of Norwegian whalers, and were impressed by the level of amenity their hosts had managed to maintain at this most remote outpost of humanity. There were electric lights and hot water; and the home of the Grytviken station manager, Fridthjof Jacobsen, was

Washing the floor

Left to right, Wordie, Cheetham, and Macklin. "I simply hate scrubbing. I am able to put aside pride of caste in most things but I must say that I think scrubbing floors is not fair work for people who have been brought up in refinement." (Lees, diary)

Grytviken Whaling Station, seen from the <u>Endurance</u>

This was the ship's last port of call before heading south towards the Weddell Sea.

not only heated but had geraniums blooming in its bow windows. These charms, however, could not conceal the noxious presence of the whaling industry: The island's natural harbors were full of greasy offal and the stench of decaying whale carcasses, and the waters of Grytviken were red.

The whalers provided the expedition with coal and clothing, bought on credit, as well as valuable information. No men on earth knew better the seas Shackleton was poised to enter, and they confirmed the reports from Buenos Aires that ice conditions were unusually severe that year, with pack extending farther north than it had in anyone's recollection. Shackleton was advised to wait until later in the austral summer, and so the brief time he had planned to spend on South Georgia turned to a full month.

The month on South Georgia appears to have been passed agreeably with the men getting to know one another and each becoming familiar with his duties. Amid the magnificent subantarctic scenery and fauna—elephant seals, penguins, and other bird life—they could at last feel their adventure to the great white south was truly under way. The dog trainers took their charges to a nearby hillside and attempted to restrain them from gorging on whale offal and rooting through the old whalers' cemetery; the scientists wandered up into the hills looking at the abundant wildlife and "securing specimens." Frank Hurley, aided by Captain Worsley and First Officer Lionel Greenstreet, lugged his forty pounds of camera equipment to the heights

Veslegard Hut, South Georgia, 28 November, 1914

Reginald James took this picture of Wordie, Hurley (holding camera bag), and Clark while on a camping trip during the monthlong sojourn on the island.

overlooking the Grytviken harbor and preserved the image of the *Endurance* riding at anchor, rendered insignificant by the stupendous encirclement of mountains. Lees, characteristically, sought to go off and climb challenging peaks on his own; Shackleton, characteristically, forbade him. The carpenter was busy constructing a covering for the extra deck space. The sailors remained with the ship.

Several members of the expedition could count themselves old Antarctic hands. Alfred Cheetham, the third officer, had been south more times than any other man on board the *Endurance* except Frank Wild: first in 1902, as boatswain on the *Morning*, the relief ship sent to search out and supply Scott's *Discovery*; as third officer with Shackleton on the *Nimrod*; and with Scott again on the *Terra Nova*. Born in Liverpool, Cheetham was small and wiry, known for his cheery, willing manner; he was the chanty-man on both the *Nimrod* and the *Endurance*, and an old salt to the marrow of his bones. When asked to join the *Nimrod* crew, so the story goes, Cheetham had immediately agreed, then hastened off to tell the wife of his mate "Chippy" Bilsby, carpenter on the *Morning*, that her husband was going to the Antarctic again. Having delivered this message, he continued to the house where Bilsby himself was working.

"Eh! Chippy lad, coom darn," Cheetham called out, in broad Liverpudlian. "Tha's barn t'ert South Pole wi me."

Bilsby: "I'se better see t'missus furst."

Cheetham: "Ah've seen t'wife, Chippy. Coom on."

Panorama of South Georgia Island, with <u>Endurance</u> in harbour

Worsley and Greenstreet, in foreground, helped Hurley lug his camera equipment up to Ducefell to take this picture.

Frank Hurley, of course, had been south as well. He was twenty-six in 1911, when he first heard word that Dr. Douglas Mawson, Australia's noted polar explorer, was planning a journey to the Antarctic. Determined to get the job of expedition photographer, but with no contacts to recommend him, Hurley had waylaid Mawson in a private railway compartment, selling himself to the explorer for the duration of their journey. Three days later, Hurley received word of his acceptance—Mawson had admired Hurley's initiative. The success of Hurley's eventual film about the Mawson expedition, entitled *Home of the Blizzard*, had partly inspired Shackleton's Imperial Trans Antarctic Film Syndicate venture. Aboard the *Endurance*, Hurley was considered "hard as nails," able to endure harsh conditions and willing to go to any length to obtain a desired shot. Professionally much admired, he was not universally liked. Having come up in the world by dint of talent and hard work, he was keenly conscious of his superior abilities. He was susceptible to flattery and was considered "rather bombastic." His nickname was "the Prince."

George Marston had been with Shackleton on the *Nimrod*. A graduate of a London art school, he was part of a young set that included Shackleton's two sisters, Helen and Kathleen, who encouraged him to apply for the position of expedition artist. On the *Nimrod* expedition, Marston took part in three sledging journeys, one of them with Shackleton, who had been impressed with Marston's physical abilities. The son of a coachmaker and grandson of a shipwright, Marston was, like Hurley, marvelously versatile—which would prove useful.

Little is known of Able Seaman Thomas McLeod, a superstitious Scotsman who had been with Scott on the *Terra Nova* and Shackleton on the *Nimrod*. Having run away to sea at the age of fourteen, he had twenty-seven years of sailing experience.

Tom Crean was a tall, raw-boned Irish seaman, one of ten children born to a farming family in a remote part of County Kerry. He had come up the ranks of the Royal Navy, having enlisted at sixteen—adding two years to his age—as a boy second class, in 1893. Fluent in Irish and English, Crean always regretted that his formal education had ceased at primary school. His own sensitivity to this fact, more than the fact itself, may have prevented him from rising higher than he did. On the *Endurance*, Crean was second officer.

But in worth, if not in actual rank, Crean was, to use Shackleton's own word, "trumps." He had gone south with Scott on both the *Discovery* and the *Terra Nova* expeditions, receiving the Albert Medal for bravery on the latter; and he had been among the sixteen who set out with Scott for the South Pole in 1911. Scott's method was to avoid assigning roles in advance, so that no one in the crew knew whether he was destined to be in the polar party, or to be turned back short of the final push, after hauling supplies for many miles. On January 3, 1912, Scott told Crean and two

Crean (standing) and Cheetham

The "Irish giant" and the diminutive "veteran of the Antarctic." Crean had sailed on the Terra Nova *and* Discovery *with Scott before joining Shackleton on the* Endurance.

companions, Lieutenant "Teddy" Evans and William Lashly, that they were to turn back the next day. Although all supplies and equipment had been rationed for two teams of four men each, at the last minute Scott chose a fifth man, "Birdie" Bowers, to join the polar party. This decision not only contributed to the demise of his own party by adding an unexpected mouth to feed, but seriously burdened the returning trio with a four-man sledging load. Evans, already suffering from scurvy, collapsed and was pulled by his companions until they could go no farther. Then, thirty-five miles from the nearest assistance, Crean set out alone with three biscuits and two sticks of chocolate.

"Well Sir, I was very weak when I reached the hut," Crean wrote in a letter to a friend. He was a hard man to rattle. Earlier in the same expedition, after an exhausting trek across fragmented sea ice with the ponies, Crean and his two companions had prepared their dinner. By mistake, a bag of curry powder was taken for cocoa. "Crean," recalled his tent mate, "drank his right down before discovering anything wrong." But tough though he was, Crean broke down and wept when, at 87° south, only 150 miles short of their goal, Scott informed him and his companions that they had not been selected for the honor of continuing with him to the pole.

A number of the sailors aboard the *Endurance* had formerly been trawlerhands in the North Sea, as brutal an occupation as could be imagined. Little suggests they were sympathetic characters, and one of them, John Vincent, previously a sailor in the navy and a trawlerhand off the coast of Iceland, would turn out to be a problematic bully. Of the two stokers, William Stephenson was a former Royal Marine and officer's servant, and Ernest Holness, the youngest of the sailors, was "a Yorkshire lad," and considered—by Lees, at any rate—to be "the most loyal to the expedition."

Four of the sailors were particularly liked. Timothy McCarthy was a young Irishman in the merchant service, known for his ebullient good humor and gift for repartee. Walter How, a Londoner, was only three weeks back home from a stint abroad when he applied for a position with the Imperial Trans-Antarctic Expedition. Shackleton was impressed with his recent experience aboard the Canadian Auxiliary Survey Ship, working only miles below the Arctic Circle off the coast of Labrador. He was also of a cheerful disposition and a good amateur artist. William Bakewell joined the expedition in Buenos Aires. He had been a farm laborer, logger, rail worker, and ranch hand in Montana before becoming a seaman at the age of twenty-seven. When his ship the *Golden Gate* ran aground in the River Plate, he and his mate Perce Black-borow wandered the docks of Buenos Aires looking for a way to England and came upon the *Endurance*.

"It was," he said, "love at first sight." On learning that she belonged to the famous polar explorer Sir Ernest Shackleton, and that he was seeking a replacement crew, the two young men presented themselves for consideration. Pleased with Bakewell's experience with sailing ships, as opposed to steam, Shackleton hired him (it may not have hurt his chances that Bakewell, the expedition's only American, posed as a Canadian,

George E. Marston
The expedition artist was described by a former shipmate as having "the frame and face of a prizefighter and the disposition of a fallen angel."

seeking a colonial's advantage). But Blackborow was turned away when Shackleton decided he had enough men. Aided by Bakewell and How, Blackborow stowed away in a clothing locker in the fo'c'sle. The day after the ship left Buenos Aires, he was discovered and dragged before Shackleton. Hungry, frightened, and seasick, the young man was subjected to an eloquent tirade from "the Boss" that impressed all onlooking seamen. In the end, Shackleton leaned close to Blackborow and said, "Do you know that on these expeditions we often get very hungry, and if there is a stow-away available he is the first to be eaten?" This was correctly interpreted as official acceptance of his presence, and Blackborow was signed on as steward to help in the galley, at £3 a month. In fact, Shackleton came to regard the quiet, conscientious Welshman as highly as any member of the crew.

One of the oldest men was Henry McNish, known by the traditional nickname for

The Endurance

ship carpenters as "Chippy." A blunt-spoken old salt from Cathcart, outside Port Glasgow, he stirred misgivings in Shackleton from the outset.

"The carpenter is the only man I am not dead certain of," Shackleton had written to his friend and agent, Ernest Perris, shortly before leaving South Georgia. McNish was perhaps the most mysterious member of the expedition. He claimed, untruthfully, to have sailed south with William Bruce's Scottish expedition in 1902, but he was in any case much travelled. For reasons that remain obscure, Shackleton and his shipmates believed him to be in his fifties, although his actual age was forty. Though not particularly liked, he was universally respected, not only as a brilliant shipwright but also as an experienced sailor in the Royal Naval Reserve.

"Chips was neither sweet-tempered nor tolerant," a shipmate from another expedition recalled. "And his Scots voice could rasp like frayed wire cable." McNish had brought along his cat, the irrepressible Mrs. Chippy, a tabby described as "full of character" by several members of the expedition, and whose chief delight was taking teasing shortcuts across the kennel roofs of the half-wild sledging dogs, whom he (for Mrs. Chippy was belatedly discovered to be a male) cannily perceived to be securely chained to their kennels.

Twenty-seven in all, not including Shackleton, the men formed a relatively small team to wage the battle south through the thousand miles of ice-strewn ocean that lay between them and their planned destination. Each must have carefully scrutinized his fellows' experience and character. Nor was Shackleton himself exempt from such assessment.

"[A] queer bird, a man of moods, & I dont know whether I like him or not," First Officer Greenstreet wrote to his father. Shackleton had arrived in Buenos Aires somewhat under the weather and does not seem to have been in top form while in South Georgia. Accompanying him on a short hike, Wordie observed that he "was troubled by a bad cough, and seemed pretty tired with the walk." Shackleton still

had much to worry about: The worst ice conditions in living memory showed no sign of improving and some of the whalers suggested that he should defer setting out until the next season. But for Shackleton postponement of the expedition would be tantamount to relinquishing it forever. Behind him lay the war and many financial loose ends.

The *Endurance* steamed out of Grytviken's Cumberland Bay on the morning of December 5, 1914. She was freshly provisioned—her cargo now included two live pigs for food—and her crew was rested and eager for the next stage of the journey. The mountains of South Georgia remained in sight until the evening, as the *Endurance* headed south by southeast. As early as the next day the ship passed numerous icebergs, and by December 7 she had encountered the outskirts of pack ice.

The Weddell Sea is uniquely configured for maximum hazard to ships. It is contained within three belts of land—the string of South Sandwich Islands to the east, the Antarctic continent proper, and the long finger of the Palmer Peninsula to the west. A prevailing current drives the roughly circular sea in a slow clockwise motion. Sea ice, which can form here during any season, is thus never dispersed into the warmer northern waters, but churned in an interminable semicircle, eventually packed by the westward drift against the Palmer Peninsula.

Worsley directing helmsman through the ice

Shielded from the wind, Worsley semaphores directions to the ship's helmsman.

For the next six weeks the *Endurance* worked its way cautiously south, dodging and weaving around loose floes and pack and sometimes smashing her way through them. Shackleton hoped that by keeping outside the pack's eastern edge, he could obliquely work his way down towards Vahsel Bay. The tactic only worked for so long, and soon he had to broach the pack.

As the *Endurance* continued south, she entered fields of snowy ice, enormous floes up to 150 square miles. "All day we have been utilizing the ship as a battering ram," Hurley wrote in his diary in mid-December. "We admire our sturdy little ship, which seems to take a delight herself in combating our common enemy, shattering the floes in grand style. When the ship comes in impact with the ice she stops, dead, shivering from truck to kelson; then almost immediately a long crack starts from our bows, into which we steam, and, like a wedge slowly force the crack sufficiently to enable a passage to be made."

Days of thick mist opened onto clear days of radiant sunshine. During the long dusk of the austral summer night the broken pack appeared to float like so many giant white water lilies on an azure pond. The ship passed crabeater seals basking on the ice and crowds of always entertaining Adélie and emperor penguins, who would pop up unexpectedly on floes and clamor at her as she passed. Gradually the bodies of open water got smaller and smaller, until the whole sea looked like a vast snowfield, broken only here and there by lanes and channels.

Christmas Day was celebrated with mince pies and Christmas pudding, colorful flags and table settings, and a singsong in the evening. Magnificent sunsets were admired from the ship's rail, and on the last day of 1914, after a difficult morning spent ramming through a bad patch of ice, the *Endurance* crossed the Antarctic Circle in a dreamlike twilight reflected in calm waters. On the night of January 1, 1915, the Scottish contingent singing "Auld Lang Syne" woke the "respectable members" who had retired for the evening. Lees peevishly noted, "Scotchmen always are a nuisance at New Year and never have voices worth speaking of." Meanwhile, on the bridge,

<u>Endurance</u> in pack ice

"Pack-ice might be described as a gigantic and interminable jigsaw puzzle devised by nature."
(*Shackleton, South*)

Shackleton, Wild, Worsley, and Hudson shook hands all around and wished each other a happy New Year.

The weather by now was usually overcast, and the *Endurance* was encountering more icebergs, grand structures that rose like fantastic sculptures of blue-white marble above the waterline, and which appeared peacock blue below it. The expedition company whiled away the time in domestic pursuits. Lees darned his socks and washed and mended his clothes; Hurley took photographs in the midnight sun. Robert Clark, the biologist, studied the diatomaceous deposits of the Weddell Sea under a microscope. On January 6, the dogs were taken off onto a convenient floe for exercise, the first they'd had since leaving South Georgia a month before; they immediately initiated one of their infamous "scraps," falling through rotten ice into the water.

Ice conditions on January 7 and 8 forced the ship to backtrack through the pack to seek a better opening, but on January 10, at 72° south, an important landmark was reached: The ship came in sight of Coats Land and began to work her way close to its great 100-foot-high wall of barrier ice. The *Endurance* was now, with fair going, as little as a week away from Vahsel Bay. With the expectation that she would still return to Buenos Aires or South Georgia for the winter, the expedition's wintering-over shore party were busy writing letters home to be carried with the returning ship.

On January 11, the ship's company began the day with a breakfast of Quaker Oats,

Berg, observed 21 December, 1914

"[A]t 10:00 a.m. we entered long leads of ice free water, in which were drifting some fine bergs of magnificent forms. One a fine cuniform mass 200 feet high, I photographed."
(*Hurley, diary*)

seal's liver, and bacon. Bad weather forced the *Endurance* to drift with a large floe. McNish, the carpenter, used this layover to make a small chest of drawers for "the Boss." Shackleton himself was observed to be looking "dead tired"; he had not slept much over the past few days. The two pigs obtained in South Georgia (named Sir Patrick and Bridget Dennis) were fattening up, and one of the dogs, Sally, had given birth to three pups; tough Tom Crean was observed with amusement to be fussing over the pups "like a hospital orderly." The day closed with a dinner of thick lentil soup, stewed clubbed seal, tinned peas, and custard.

January 12 dawned with mist and snow, but was otherwise a good day. Clark bagged interesting specimens in his dredge nets and towards evening a flock of young emperor penguins was passed on a nearby floe. The *Endurance*, now under steam, broke from the pack ice into open water and reached the bay that marked the farthest south of William Bruce's *Scotia* expedition in 1903. Shallow soundings of

The upper deck after a light snow fall

"It is wonderful how the dogs prefer to sleep on the snow covered deck rather than in their kennels." (Lees, diary)

January 6, 1915; Exercising the dogs

"During the day the dogs were taken for a run on the large floe to which we were anchored. The exercise did them a great deal of good—it being the first they have had for nearly a month." (Hurley, diary)

Crean with pups
"Opposite the pigs are 5 puppies & their mother, the 'interesting event' having taken place three days ago, but so far Tom Crean, who has cared for her like a hospital orderly is the only one who has seen the little creatures, though we all hear their shrill little squeaks. They will soon be fun." (Lees, diary)

about 150 fathoms indicated the proximity of land. Lees, busy amid the stores, triumphantly rooted out "a case of marmalade and one or two other things that Sir Ernest especially wanted."

On January 13, after skirting heavy pack around the barrier all night, the *Endurance* was again drifting within the floes, which showed no sign of opening up. For two hours she searched for an opening, then banked her fires and lay to. The following day, January 14, the ship was still held fast. The weather was magnificent, however, the best since leaving South Georgia, with the temperature at 25° Fahrenheit. Hurley, ever on the lookout for photogenic scenes, described the surroundings thus:

> The bergs & floes were reflected in the deep blue water, while the heavy pressure ice, gleaming in the sunshine with its deep blue shadows, was one of the finest sights I have seen in the South. The ice was more like serracs than pack ice, for it was so tossed, broken & crushed. Great pressure ridges thrown up 15 to 20 feet in height bear evidence of the terrific force & pressure of the ice in these latitudes.

From the crow's nest high above the ship, Lees noted that tremendous pressure pack could be seen in every direction.

Yet, in the evening, a rising breeze began to work upon the pack, and before

Laying to, 14 January, 1915

"Tied up all day to the floe ice. . . . The day was magnificent. The finest day since leaving South Georgia
& in fact the second sunny one we have had." (*Hurley, diary*)

14 January, 1915

"This ice was more like serracs than pack ice for it was so tossed, broken & crushed. Great pressure ridges thrown up 15 to 20 feet in height bear evidence of the terrific force & pressure of the ice in these latitudes."
(*Hurley, diary*)

14 January, 74° 10′S 27° 10′W

The lay-to in the floe ice allowed the crew to take excursions on the ice.

Pack ice, January 20, 1915

Taken the day the Endurance *was finally held by the ice. "We have only 85 miles to go but the wind is still
from NE & keeping the ice hard against the barrier." (McNish, diary)*

Endurance beset, full sail

On the night of January 24, a lead of open water appeared ahead of the ship. "Today at 9 a.m. we hoisted all sail & got up full steam and continued to drive the engines full speed ahead until noon in the hopes of reaching the open water but all to no avail." (Lees, diary) midnight a lane of open water had appeared at the foot of the barrier. In the early morning of January 15, the *Endurance* continued under hazy skies. An unusually large number of seals were seen throughout the day, and at three in the afternoon the ship passed a large group swimming out from the barrier to offshore pack. The whole company gathered at the rail to watch and exclaim as the seals dove and played around the ship like porpoises—it was an event that everyone remembered with affection. By evening, the skies were clear and a lane of water had opened to allow the *Endurance* to speed south under sail. Fine, clear water lay ahead. Just before midnight, in the strange perpetual summer twilight, the ship came upon a sheltered bay formed by the projecting end of a great glacier and the ice barrier.

"The bay . . . would have made an excellent landing-place," Shackleton wrote, noting its "natural quay" of flat ice and its unusual configuration, which sheltered it from all but northerly winds. "I named the place Glacier Bay," he continued, "and had reason later to remember it with regret."

The *Endurance* steamed along the glacier front through the night, and by early morning had arrived at another glacial overflow, deeply crevassed, its frozen torrent spilling over a cliff face that rose as high as 350 feet. At 8:30 a.m., the ship's splendid run of 124 miles was brought to a halt by dense pack ice, partly held in place, as Shackleton surmised, by the strikingly large bergs in the vicinity. The ship drew up close to a small berg distinguished by well-defined bands of embedded matter, which expedition geologist James Wordie identified as "biotite granite." Later in the day, an easterly wind blew up, eventually increasing to gale force. While the leeward pack began to break and disperse under its pressure, the *Endurance* lay to behind a convenient berg. It was tedious to be held up after such a satisfying run. Lees, for one, whiled away the time with a characteristic tidying up of stores in the hold.

The gale continued throughout the following day. The *Endurance*, unanchored, pitched about in the rough sea, steaming around and around in small circles all the while. A few seals rode the waves past her, their heads high above the water. From his bunk, Hurley looked up from his book to glance at the huge white bergs and lowering clouds through a porthole window.

On January 18, the gale had abated sufficiently to allow the *Endurance* to raise sail in the morning and take advantage of a long lead that had opened at the foot of the glacier front. Pack ice was encountered, however, in the afternoon. Cautiously, the *Endurance* was nosed through the thick brash into open water, where she enjoyed a twenty-four-mile run before heading into more heavy brash and large, loose floes.

"The character of the pack has again changed," Worsley noted. "The floes are very thick but are composed of a greater proportion of snow; tho' they are broken up slightly into large floes the brash between is so thick & heavy that we cannot push thro' except with a very great expenditure of power. . . . We therefore prefer to lie to for a while to see if the pack opens up at all when this NE wind clears."

Fighting seasickness brought on by the rough sea, Lees had endured his turn at the wheel, where it was "snowing and blowing and generally horrid." In the afternoon he spent his spare time readying the stores for landing, sorting them into "ship" and "shore" piles. Less industrious members of the expedition were bored by the delay.

"It is gratifying to feel we are only 80 miles from our intended base, Vahsel Bucht," Hurley wrote, referring to it by its German name. "We are all keen to reach it as the monotony is telling on some of us."

The weather on the following morning was good, but the ice conditions had worsened, the pack having closed in around the ship during the night. The scientists dutifully took specimens, but everyone's attention was on the ice. The gale had packed it so tightly against the continental shelf that no water at all could now be sighted from the crow's nest. Still, the ship's company turned in that night hoping that a change in the wind would open the pack and allow them to continue on their way. The *Endurance* was now as little as one good day's sail away from Vahsel Bay.

The northeasterly gale that had been blowing intermittently since January 16 rose again in the course of the night. The day broke dull and snowy, revealing the pack pressed around the ship more densely than before. Still, the temperature was mild, 28° Fahrenheit, so as Lees noted "there is no fear, at present, our getting frozen in." With nowhere to go, there was not much to do. The day's excitement came when Frank Wild shot a nine-foot crabeater seal, providing fresh meat for the men and dogs and Mrs. Chippy. The scientists held a singsong in Clark's cabin, a favorite gathering place as it was close to the boilers. Hurley continued writing letters to be taken with the ship when she returned to South Georgia Island, and Lees busied himself with washing and mending his wardrobe.

The gale was still blowing from the northeast on January 21, drifting snow from the continental ice shelf; consequently the air was full of moisture, and the wardroom and cabins became damp with condensation. Ice pressure against the rudder caused grave concern, and the crew went over the side to chip it clear. Although it represented a costly expenditure of fuel, Shackleton kept steam up in the boilers so that the ship could take advantage of the least opening in the pack. Held fast in the ice, the *Endurance* was being carried with the rest of the pack by the Weddell Sea's current; soon she would be moving away from land.

After six days of blowing on and off, the northeasterly gale subsided on January 22, and the following day dawned sunny and calm. Hurley immediately took advantage

of the light to take some color photographs, and Lees continued his scrubbing and darning. An assessment of the ship's supply of fuel determined that only 75 tons of coal remained of the 160 the *Endurance* had carried from South Georgia.

At midnight on January 24, a rent in the surrounding ice opened a lead at right angles to the ship—but 100 yards distant. Full steam and sail were raised, but the *Endurance* could not ram through, and the ship's company took to the ice with chisels and crowbars to try to hack a path to the tantalizing lane to freedom. Although the ice could be seen breaking up some distance ahead, around the ship herself they could do nothing.

"Held up in the ice. Nothing of any movement takes place"; "still fast & no signs of any opening"; "the lead that promised so much has almost closed up again"; "still fast"—thus, in this anticlimactic way, do the diary entries over the next few days indicate the men's dawning awareness that the decision to lay to in the pack—made, it seems in retrospect, almost casually on the night of January 18—had proved fatal to their plans.

"It appears as though we have stuck fast for this season," Hurley wrote at the close of January 27. "A noticeable drop in the temperature at midnight, +9 being recorded. This has had the effect of freezing up many of the small pools & cementing together the floes, an ominous happening."

Playing football on the ice
A popular diversion while the ship was held up. Macklin and Clark, both Scots, were recognized as the most outstanding players. The teams were Port watch versus Starboard watch.

Daily depth soundings indicated that the ship was drifting farther and farther away from land. With the regular routine winding down and less work for everyone to do, boredom inevitably set in. Games of football on the ice and attention to the dogs provided some diversion. In the wardroom, the scientists amused one another by reading aloud in the evening, and Sunday singsongs were a regular event. Saturday nights the traditional toast was drunk "to our sweethearts and wives" (followed unfailingly by the chorus, "may they never meet"), a ritual overdone by McNish one night, resulting in a quarrelsome disturbance in the fo'c'sle.

Although scientists and sailors had been prepared to travel south together, they had not counted on sharing one another's company for a polar winter. And while the possibility of the ship's wintering over had been discussed in Buenos Aires, the original plan had called for her to return to safe haven after depositing the shore party and their supplies.

"The idea of spending the winter in an ice bound ship is extremely unpleasant," Hurley wrote in early February, "more so, owing to the necessarily cramping of the work and the forced association with the ships party—who, although being an amiable crowd are not altogether partial to the scientific staff."

False hopes arose several times with the appearance of a lane, or a change in the ice, and more than once the men set out to cut or shake the ship free. On February 22, the drift of the *Endurance* carried her to the 77th parallel. It would be the farthest

Cutting the ice around <u>Endurance</u>

On February 14 and 15, 1915, a lead of free water appeared 400 yards ahead of the stricken ship, and the crew made strenuous efforts to cut a path to this tantalizing lane.

Trying to break up ice from around <u>Endurance</u>

"The actual cutting out of the ice with picks & saws is difficult enough but lifting the blocks, some of which weigh as much as 3 and 4 hundred weight, out of the water, hauling them away, breaking them up . . . entails much hard work."

(Lees, diary)

south attained by the Imperial Trans-Antarctic Expedition.

"The summer had gone," Shackleton wrote. "Indeed the summer had scarcely been with us at all. . . . [T]he seals were disappearing and the birds were leaving us. The land showed still in fair weather on the distant horizon, but it was beyond our reach now." On February 24, Shackleton ordered the cessation of ship routine, and the *Endurance* officially became a winter station.

Having battled valiantly through 1,000 miles of pack ice in six weeks, the *Endurance* had come within a single day's journey of her landing base. Now exhausted by futile attempts to cut their ship free, Shackleton and his men could only watch helplessly as the *Endurance*'s drift carried them out of sight of land. The fateful turn of events affected no one more than Shackleton. Not only was he burdened with the responsibility of keeping his diverse company in good health and spirits throughout a polar winter, but he had to swallow bitter personal disappointment. He was forty years old, and the *Endurance* expedition had taken formidable energy to assemble. With a war under way at home, it was unlikely that he would have another opportunity of returning to the south anytime soon; this was his last shot. Although for some while it remained theoretically possible that the expedition could proceed in the spring, when the breakup of the pack would release his ship, Shackleton was realistic enough to know that every passing day made this increasingly impossible.

"It was more than tantalizing, it was maddening," wrote Alexander Macklin, one of the ship's two surgeons, in his diary. "Shackleton at this time showed one of his sparks of real greatness. He did not rage at all, or show outwardly the slightest sign of disappointment; he told us simply and calmly that we must winter in the Pack, explained its dangers and possibilities; never lost his optimism, and prepared for Winter."

Meanwhile, Huberht Hudson, the navigator, repeatedly tried the ship's wireless to get signals from the Falklands, the nearest transmitting stations, but without success. The expedition was not only out of sight of land. No one in the world knew where it was.

"All hands again attack the ice and we work the ship a third of the way to the lead ahead."
(Hurley, diary)

**Trying to free the
Endurance**

"All hands hard at it till midnight when a survey is made of the remaining ⅔, some 400 yards. It is reluctantly determined to relinquish the task as the remainder of the ice is unworkable."
(Hurley, diary)

<u>Endurance</u> in the ice
Hurley noted that the pack frequently resembled a billowing sea.

A midsummer sunset, February 1915
"It was a charming evening. The atmosphere was charged with a redundancy of shimmering frost crystals."
(Hurley, diary)

The ship caught in a pressure crack. 19 October 1915

"For the moment it seemed the ship would be thrown on her beam ends. Secured several fine photographs of our Gallant ship." (Hurley, diary)

The Breakup

March opened with a blizzard and a temperature of –8° Fahrenheit. The floes around the ship had become so rough from the wind working upon them that crew members smashed two sledges trying to haul seal meat over the broken surface. Towards the end of this same day, Worsley gave orders for all hands to stay on board. The snow had become so heavy that it was dangerous to stray outside.

When the weather cleared, the creaking of ice and the sounds of the wind in all its moods filled the silence. At night, the men were kept awake by the light glinting upon the floes throughout the long austral twilight. Realistically, one could not expect the breakup of the ice until spring, sometime in October—some seven months away.

According to Shackleton's original plan, the shore party, composed of scientists and sledgers, would have been busy working at their various duties, preparing for the journeys they would undertake come spring. Those who were to have remained with the ship would have been working their passage back to a winter haven. But now the jobs the men had come to do could not be done, and the danger of a numbing tedium hung over them. From his own experience Shackleton well knew the peculiar psychological strain of the eerie silence and black emptiness of the impending Antarctic winter.

To guard against this, he set a strict winter routine. Instead of the usual rotation of sea watches, a single watchman was on duty from 8 p.m. to 8 a.m., allowing all other hands to enjoy uninterrupted sleep. To boost morale as much as stave off the cold, Shackleton issued to all hands the winter clothing originally designated for the shore parties (each article of which Lees had assiduously catalogued in his diary): two Jaeger wool shirts and combinations, or long underwear, Shetland wool mitts,

one Shetland wool jersey, and, most important, Burberry tunics and trousers. These last were, in the words of one expedition member, roughly the weight of umbrella fabric, or calico, but supposedly so tightly woven as to be impervious to wind. A number of the sailors immediately stowed the new clothing safely away in their lockers, so as to have it "for swank" when they returned to civilization. Only clothing meant for the transcontinental party was kept apart, in the belief, or pretext, that the crossing might still happen.

Shackleton's immediate concern was to establish comfortable winter quarters for his men. March temperatures were running from +11° to −24°, and the deckhouse cabins where the afterguard of scientists and ship officers lived were bitterly cold. Shackleton ordered the storage area between decks cleared, and Chippy McNish began the work of constructing cubicles within this more insulated area. On March 11, the men moved down to their new quarters, which they had christened "the Ritz." Each of the roughly six-by-five-foot cubicles housed two men, and each received a wry name from its occupants, such as "The Billabong," "The Anchorage," "The Sailors Rest." In the middle of the space was a long table where all meals were taken, and a bogie stove stood at one end. The Ritz was not only warm; its close quarters seemed familial and cozy. Crean, Wild, Marston, and Worsley moved into the old wardroom, while the sailors remained in the fo'c'sle, which was situated between decks and so sufficiently insulated. Shackleton also stayed where he was, alone in the Captain's cabin, aft; it was the coldest part of the ship. Winter accommodations for the non-human members were also effected. The dogs were housed in ice block kennels dubbed "dogloos" in an extended circle around the ship. The pigs were disembarked to similar winter quarters, which the sailors called "pigloos"; Mrs. Chippy stayed on board the ship.

Ship's cabin, <u>Endurance</u>
Shackleton's cabin, the tidy repository of his ambitions.

The nights lengthened, and by the end of March there were equal hours of light and darkness. The fifty-odd dogs, big, energetic, wild, and playful, became the objects of intense interest and amusement. Their care occupied several hours a day, while their antics and different personalities kept the men on their toes. The animals took well to the ice, sleeping through blizzards with equanimity, curled in furry balls under the snow.

"When they think there is a danger of their being overlooked by their human pals," wrote Worsley, "they sit up, shake themselves, do a song & dance & then coil down again for another snooze til GRUB—all our dogs spell it that way."

In early April, Shackleton divided the dogs into six teams assigned to specific

The way to the lead
A line of ice mounds were thrown up, linked with light rope to serve as guidance during blizzards.

Kennels around the ship

"Dogs all placed on shore much to their delight. All hands engaged building Igloos or Dogloos, from ice blocks & snow. . . . The dogs are secured by chain, one end of which is buried in the ice & frozen therein." (Hurley, diary)

Macklin and Greenstreet boiling blubber for dogs

A number of ice structures, including a quarantine and hospital for sick dogs, formed the dogloo complex.

minders, each of whom came to regard his charges with intense proprietary pride. Rivalries and races between the teams now provided further entertainment ("My team is one of the best," Hurley characteristically confided to his diary). The dogs' health was a matter of constant concern. A number had already died, the victims of intestinal worms. April was also a tragic month for the pigs, whom the seamen converted into pork.

In the dwindling light, the men exercised the dog teams, or scouted for now infrequent seals, or went off on exploratory hikes across the ice. Like the hapless *Endurance*, a number of icebergs had also become trapped in the pack, and so ship and landscape drifted in tandem, held together by the northwest current. As familiar objects in the men's erratically shifting world, many of these companion icebergs came to be regarded with affection. Notable among these was the aptly named Rampart Berg, which they had first encountered in early January, while still under sail.

Some 150 feet in height, it now reared majestically above the ice twenty miles from the ship.

In the evenings, there were singsongs for entertainment, led by Leonard Hussey, the popular meteorologist who was also a proficient banjo player. Occasionally, Hurley presented lantern slide lectures, showing scenes of ice and snow from his Mawson expedition, or of sun and vegetation from his trip to Java. After most of the company turned in to bed, the lone night watchman was often joined by his pals, sharing such treats as cocoa and sardines on toast; these night visitors were called "ghosts."

On the first of May, the sun disappeared entirely, not to be seen for the next four months. The men's activities were now curtailed even more. Exercise of the dogs continued, despite the difficulty in navigating the sledges over broken ice in the uncertain light, but excursions far from the ship were discouraged. Diversions of all kinds were sought: Hurley and Hussey became keen chess opponents, welcoming the mental stimulation of the game. In the fo'c'sle, the sailors played cards and draughts. Books were read and argumentatively analyzed, and for a time guessing games were all the rage in the Ritz. In late May, the men succumbed to winter madness, shaving their heads and posing amid great hilarity while Hurley immortalized the moment with a photograph.

Yet even in these winter months, there were days and nights of intense, magical beauty that raised morale and reminded some of the men why they had ventured into this harsh world. The strange mingling of faint daylight and a radiant moon on the frozen sea rendered the landscape mystically luminous. In the pure dark of a clear night, the stars glittered with unimagined brilliance, while faint aurorae tinged the horizon. Coming back from a sledging ride one night, Hurley described with elation the sensation of driving into the face of the moon.

The diaries of the men reflect, to varying degrees, a generally contented company. There are notes of peevishness and signs of the strain of living at close quarters with the same faces day after day, but no friction of real consequence.

"We all manage to live very happily here on board in spite of conflicting interests

Self (Hurley) giving a "lantern chat"

"Hurley gives a lantern slide show of New Zealand. Having the honour of being the only New Zealander aboard, I do my best to give a lecture which consists mainly of 'This is such & such a place.' Tap tap with a stick for the next picture. At the conclusion I give an imitation of a Maori haka or war dance with 3 or 4 excellent pupils."
(Worsley, diary)

and the fact that most members are what one might term rather definite personalities and of somewhat different stations in life," wrote Lees, ever mindful of class distinctions. Yet, he continues, "[T]here is no real need to have quarrels of any kind with one's comrades. Amongst gentlemen quarrels should be and can be avoided and there is no reason therefore why that should not be the case down here." This was a particularly generous statement, written as it was only a short time after Hussey and Hurley had emptied a handful of lentils into his open mouth while he slept, to stop his snoring.

The general peace that prevailed on the *Endurance* had not come about by accident and owed something to the manner in which Shackleton had selected the men in the first place. When James presented himself for his interview, the great explorer had bewildered him by asking not about his suitability for a major polar expedition, or details of his scientific work—but whether he could sing.

"Oh, I don't mean any Caruso stuff," Shackleton had continued, "but I suppose you can shout a bit with the boys?" The question proved to be uncannily appropriate. What he was looking for was an "attitude," not paper qualifications.

Shackleton's presence informed every event that occurred on his ship. On the one hand, he was always ready to be one of the boys: He shaved his head along with everyone else, and he joined, enthusiastically and tunelessly, in the singsongs. He was

A morning in the Ritz, midwinter 1915

At left rear, Blackborow carries a lump of ice to be melted for water. Right, the scientists work.

Hussey and Hurley (Nightwatch) indulge in a friendly game

"Hussey & I are night watchmen. During the night we indulge in a game of chess. We are both keen enthusiasts & it exercises one's otherwise stagnant intellect." (Hurley, diary)

anxious, with much to ponder and plan, but he did not require a brooding solitude in which to do this. He was always among his men, perceived to be in good spirits, and this fact alone was in great part responsible for the atmosphere of security that pervaded their stricken circumstances.

Shackleton did not believe in unnecessary discipline, and yet ultimately nothing happened without his consent. He was known to be above all fair, and so commands were obeyed not only because they were commands, but because they were generally perceived as being reasonable. His attention to the crew in the fo'c'sle was scrupulous. This was illustrated very clearly when the winter clothing was distributed. The fo'c'sle hands were supplied first, before officers and the shore party: "Whoever goes short it is not the crew," Worsley wrote.

Walter How and William Bakewell, both lowly able seamen but avid readers, could look forward to discussing the books they had read in the excellent ship's library one-on-one with Sir Ernest Shackleton. Blackborow, the stowaway, was made to attend to his schooling, Sir Ernest having taken a personal interest in the bright, conscientious young man. Yet when occasion required, Shackleton's commanding personality could also confront the most difficult individuals head on. John Vincent, the bosun, a swaggering trawlerhand who was physically bigger and stronger than any of the rest of the crew, was a bully. When a delegation from the fo'c'sle complained to Shackleton of ill treatment at his hands, the Boss summoned Vincent to his cabin. Vincent left shaken and demoted, and caused no more specific trouble. Shackleton had not felt the need for backup in this encounter, which in the hands of lesser men could have turned into an unpleasantly jittery affair.

"He could put on a look, a disdainful look that made you shrivel up," according to First Officer Lionel Greenstreet. "He could be very cutting when he wanted to, but I think it was more the look."

Above all else, Shackleton judged a man by the degree of optimism he projected. "Optimism," Shackleton once said, "is true moral courage." Those not blessed with this gift he regarded with transparent contempt. This was the case with poor Lees, who was probably the most universally unpopular member of the expedition on account of his snobbishness and his inclination to be absent when hard work was demanded. For Shackleton, however, these flaws mattered less than Lees's naked anxiety about supplies and provisions. Lees had been appointed storekeeper and was in charge of rationing and keeping tally of what was consumed; but his able fulfillment of these duties was marred by his tendency to hoard and secret away trivial odds and ends for his own personal use. This, to Shackleton, suggested morbid pessimism, a lack of faith in availability of future stores. And so, despite Lees's own reverence for Shackleton as a leader, he was despised.

Characteristically, however, Shackleton was not vindictive. When, later in the winter, Lees was laid up with a bad back after shovelling snow ("the first work he has done since we left London," McNish sourly observed), Shackleton placed him in his own cabin, checking in on him from time to time and bringing him cups of tea.

"At first," wrote Lees plaintively, "I was in my own bunk lying in indifference & almost complete darkness all day. . . ." These are the words of a lonely man. One has the distinct feeling that Shackleton sensed some less observable malaise behind Lees's symptoms, and that he whisked Lees away from self-pity and the needling of his skeptical shipmates for a little ego boosting—all for a man he actively disliked.

Another pillar of the high morale on board *Endurance* was Frank Wild, Shackleton's second-in-command. No man had a bad word to say about him. "He has," wrote Lees, "rare tact and the happy knack of saying nothing and yet getting people to do things just as he requires them. . . . [I]f he has any orders to give us he gives them in the nicest way." Wild was forty, the same age as Shackleton. He was born in Yorkshire, the son of a schoolteacher, and claimed, untruly, that he was a direct descendant of the great Captain Cook. Before his first journey south on the *Discovery*, Wild had served in both the merchant service and the navy. He later declined Scott's invitation to join the *Terra Nova* expedition, casting his lot instead with Mawson's Australasian Antarctic Expedition. Wild had a laid-back competence, an unassuming manner, and it was to him that most petty complaints were made—that Clark, the biologist, wasn't polite enough, that Marston was a bully. To each grievance Wild appeared to give complete attention and understanding, with the result that the petitioner left feeling vindicated, even if no action was actually taken. Wild's loyalty to Shackleton was bone-marrow deep, and together the two men made a formidably efficient team.

Despite the efforts to generate amusements, time hung very heavy for the scientists. James "Jock" Wordie, the geologist, and Reginald "Jimmy" James, the magnetician and physicist, had been friends at Cambridge. Jimmy James, earnest and reserved, was the stereotypical academic, brilliant and engaged in his field, somewhat baffled and inept in everything outside of it. The son of a London umbrella maker, James had led a sheltered academic life. He had given up a desirable university appointment to come south (his ice-block physics lab was called a "physloo" by the

R. W. James

"James was physicist, and was engaged in working magnetic observations, occultations of stars. . . . He had some wonderful electrical machines which none of us understood, and a joke of ours that annoyed him very much, was that he did not either." (Macklin, diary)

Worsley, James take observations during the winter

"Worsley and James had a large telescope which they set up, and by getting the exact moment of occultation of certain stars, were able to work out the exact time."
(*Macklin, diary*)

sailors). James was a good conversationalist, talking excitedly about such issues as vaporization, pressure of gases, and atmospheric phenomena—often baited by Greenstreet and Hudson, whose facetious questions would eventually silence him. Unexpectedly, he proved to be one of the best actors in the farcical skits that were a mainstay of ship entertainment.

Wordie was from Glasgow, and a popular member of the expedition. His dry humor and unmalicious leg pulling were much appreciated. He had determined to join the expedition while at Cambridge, despite having attended a dinner there with Lady Scott, Captain Robert Scott's colorful widow, who "tried to dissuade all would be candidates from the thought of going" with Shackleton. But Wordie suspected that this would be the "last big expedition which would go South." Unable to do much in the way of geology, he had turned his attention to glaciology.

Robert Clark, the biologist, was a dour man of very few words; even in Hurley's photographs, his reserve and self-containment are unmistakable. He won respect from all hands, being hardworking and strong, and could be counted on to volunteer for disagreeable jobs such as shovelling coal; he was also an excellent football player. Almost from the moment he left England, he was at work with his dredging nets, and grimly continued with his scientific duties while in the ice. He was forever skinning and dissecting penguins, a practice that gave rise to the rumor among the sailors that the scientists were looking for gold in the animals' stomachs.

Leonard Hussey, the meteorologist, was a Londoner by birth, and his shipmates amused themselves by teasing him for being a "cockney." Having taken his degree from London University, he worked in the Sudan as an archaeologist before joining the *Endurance*; Shackleton claimed to have chosen him because the improbability of a man travelling from the heart of Africa to Antarctica amused him. Hussey's dedication to science was perhaps not as strong as that of his companions.

"The vagaries of the climate quite bewilder Hussey," Lees observed. "For just when he thinks it is going to do one thing the precise opposite happens."

The two surgeons on board, Alexander Macklin and James McIlroy, were kept
busy with the dogs: Both had been appointed as sledging team drivers, and it was
their lot to attend to the parasite-ridden animals. Macklin was a Scot, the son of a

**A man checking an ice hole
outside the ship**

*Probably Clark, who persisted
with dredging for specimens
throughout the period on the ice.*

physician from the Scilly Isles: Much of his boy-
hood had been spent around the islands in small
boats. Although he could be quick-tempered, he
was generally soft-spoken and very hardworking.
He was also considered one of the group's best
rugby players. McIlroy was about thirty-five
years old, handsome and sardonic, already a man
of the world who had practiced for years in
Egypt, Malaya, and Japan and as ship's doctor on
East Indian passenger steamers. He was from
Northern Ireland (a third of the expedition were
Scotch and Irish), and his humor could be
wicked. One of his most successful perfor-
mances—as reported by Lees himself—was
an imitation of Lees's excessive deference to
Shackleton:

> [McIlroy:] (Dancing about in a most effu-
> sive way) "Yes sir, oh yes certainly sir, sar-
> dines sir, yes sir here they are (dashes to
> pantry and back) and bread sir, oh yes sir,
> bread sir, you shall have the night watch-
> man's bread sir." (Another dash to the
> pantry and much groveling effusion and so
> on) "And may I black your boots sir," . . .

In the fo'c'sle, the sailors spent a great deal of
their time in their beds.

"They just sleep the time away as best they can and never seem to look for any
occupation," Lees wrote, disapprovingly. The sailors were exempt from night watch
duties, and although they had to tend to their own quarters, they were not called
upon to help out in the Ritz. Again, Shackleton's care was to ensure that no one in
the lower deck had cause to feel aggrieved. There had been hints that they could
be troublesome, principally on the issue of meals. Though seal and penguin meat
were routinely served in the wardroom, grumbling resistance to this had arisen in
the fo'c'sle on the grounds that serving seal, as opposed to costly tinned meat, was
"a ——— cheap way of running the expedition." But their prejudices were catered
to only so far. The word came down from the fo'c'sle one afternoon that one of the
sailors had not found the day's menu of Heinz Spaghetti in Tomato to his taste.

The night watchman's visitors

The night watchman's duties consisted of keeping alight the fires in the Ritz, upper-deck wardroom, fo'c'sle, and Shackleton's cabins, and keeping an eye on the dogs in the event that they "came adrift." Above all, he was expected to watch for signs of change in the ice.

A glimpse in the fo'c'sle

*Conjectured in background,
How with ukulele, Stephenson
beside him; around table (left to
right), Holness, Vincent,
Blackborow, McLeod.*

Shackleton sent word back that he himself had been brought up to eat what was put in front of him.

Louis Rickinson and Alfred Kerr, the two engineers, were both so quiet and unassuming that their shipmates knew little about either of them, although both were admired for their efficiency and tidiness. Rickinson, who was in his thirties, was distinguished for his experience with internal combustion engines—and for being particularly sensitive to the cold. Kerr, who was a little over twenty, had worked on large oil tank steamers.

Possibly no one had less to do than the three men responsible for moving the *Endurance* forward. Frank Worsley, the captain, was now for all intents and purposes a man without a ship. Worsley was from an educated family of settlers who had come to New Zealand from England (his father had attended Rugby). He had grown up living the rugged, outdoor life of a pioneer, and at sixteen had followed his brother to sea, as an apprentice on a wool clipper. After coming up through the ranks of the merchant service, he eventually moved to England and joined the Royal Naval Reserve. Rambunctious and erratic, he was much like some of the high-spirited sledging dogs. One of the reasons Shackleton had reconsidered his plan to return the *Endurance* to safe haven over the winter was that he did not completely trust Worsley to deliver her safely the following season without supervision. Few men so thoroughly enjoyed all aspects of the expedition in all its extremes as Frank Worsley.

He was fond of claiming that his cabin was too stuffy, and slept instead in the 0° passageway; he relished shocking his shipmates by taking snow baths on the ice. His diaries are anecdotal, with a keen eye for situational comedy and for the beauty of the landscape around him. Like Shackleton, he was a romantic, dreamily in search of buried treasure, of improbable journeys. Yet for all Worsley's impracticalities, he was an expertly skilled sailor. Before moving to England, he served for several years in the New Zealand Government Steamer Service, a time spent mostly in the Pacific, where he learned to sail small boats in heavy surf.

Lionel Greenstreet, a young officer in the merchant service, between commissions, had signed on to the *Endurance* at short notice— twenty-four hours before the ship sailed from Plymouth—when the original first officer withdrew to join the war effort. His father was a respected captain in the New Zealand Shipping Company. Perceptive, critical, and a hard worker, he chose as companions the taciturn Clark and the rather superior Frank Hurley.

Huberht Hudson, the navigator, was the son of a minister and had grown up in an educated family, but in a tough East End neighborhood. He had left a school sponsored by the Worshipful Company of Carpenters at age fourteen, to be apprenticed at Trinity House. He was a "mate" in the merchant service, but was studying hard for his "master" rank while on the *Endurance*. He was regarded by his shipmates as extraordinarily good-hearted and unselfish, although at times a bit "touched."

"One never quite knows," wrote Lees, "whether he is on the brink of a mental breakdown or bubbling over with suppressed intellectuality." He earned the nickname "Buddha" after appearing in a bedsheet with a kettle lid tied to his head at a small costume party held early in the expedition on board the ship. He was also the most proficient catcher of penguins for the ship larder.

A handful of men kept busy despite the expedition's setback. Charles Green, the cook, and Blackborow, the steward, worked hard in the galley from early morning until night, preparing meals for twenty-eight men. Green was the son of a master

Hudson with young Emperor Penguin chicks, 12 January 1915; Lat. 74° 45S, 22.33W

The navigator became renowned for his penguin-catching skills.

Cook skinning a penguin in the galley

On the Endurance, *Green's day began at dawn and ended only after dinner. The son of a pastry chef, he baked twelve loaves of bread a day, in addition to skinning and preparing game captured on the ice.*

baker, and had run away to sea at the age of twenty-one, becoming a cook in the Merchant Navy. When war broke out, he joined a Royal Mail Line passenger liner, which docked in Buenos Aires around the time Shackleton was cleaning house. Hearing that the *Endurance* cook had been sacked, Green applied for the job; he had in fact met Worsley once before, in Sardinia. Blackborow, the eldest of nine children, grew up in Newport, Wales, near the town's active docks in a seafaring family. A hint of temper, the capability of plainly speaking his mind, was perceived to lurk beneath his pleasant, easygoing manner. At only twenty, he was the youngest member of the crew.

Chippy McNish was also rarely idle. He was not merely a carpenter, but a master craftsman and shipwright, and was constantly building or adapting things—card tables, chests of drawers, dog kennels, decking.

"All the work he did was first class," according to his shipmate Macklin. He was never seen to take measurements: He simply looked at his job, then went away and cut the pieces, which always fit perfectly. Even Lees, who loathed him, recognized that McNish was "an expert wooden ship's man." Although neither an officer nor a scientist, McNish was officially one of the afterguard, and his quarters were therefore not in the fo'c'sle, but in the wardroom, now relocated to the Ritz. For the fastidious Lees, eating at the same table with so unrefined a person was a kind of penance ("at scooping up peas with a knife he is a perfect juggler"). Lees would have been taken aback to learn McNish's views of the propriety of the shore party, of which he, Lees, was a member: "I have been shipmates with all sorts of men," McNish confided to his diary, "both in sail & steam but never nothing like some of our shore party as the most filthy langue is used as terms of endearment & worse than all is tolerated." This from an old salt whose blunt-spoken manner intimidated nearly everyone else.

Between McNish and Worsley there was likewise little love lost, McNish holding a very low and undisguised opinion of Worsley's high jinks and erratic ways. Not one of the expedition company could have guessed, in these early months of the winter of 1915, that the lives of the company would eventually depend upon the skills of these two men — the rambunctious captain and the gruff, uncouth Chippy McNish.

Finally, Frank Hurley's work remained unaffected by the change in plans. An able handyman, he kept continually busy with self-imposed tasks, such as creating an efficient "thaw box" for frozen seal meat, or carving signs for the various Ritz cubicles; his stint as an electrician in a Sydney post office enabled him to run the *Endurance*'s little electric plant. But above all, he was occupied with his photography. Hurley's images from the earliest days of the expedition, when the *Endurance* first entered the pack ice, are marvelous, bold, abstract patterns shaped by the play of ship's mast against ice, or the cross formed by mast and yard arm against a lead of

"Frank Hurley"
"Hurley, our photographer, is an interesting character. He is Australian—very Australian & was photographer on Sir Douglas Mawson's recent Australasian Antarctic expedition to Adelie Land. As a photographer he excels & I doubt if his work could be equalled even by Ponting. . . ."
(Lees, diary)

open water. They reflect what must have been the heady sensation of having the whole of Antarctica as a bare, white canvas to be etched by the stark, clean lines of the *Endurance* and her shadow.

"H is a marvel," Worsley wrote towards the end of January. "[W]ith cheerful Australian profanity he perambulates alone aloft & everywhere, in the most dangerous & slippery places he can find, content & happy at all times but cursing so if he can get a good or novel picture. Stands bare & hair waving in the wind, where we are gloved & helmeted, he snaps his snaps or winds his handle turning out curses of delight & pictures of Life by the fathom."

Once the *Endurance* became trapped, Hurley turned his camera to both the domestic life of the ship, and to the vision of it improbably suspended in the protean world

Hurley

This photograph shows Hurley with both his still and his movie film cameras.

of the ice. On duty at all hours of the day or night, sometimes arising at midnight to take photographs, he was keenly sensitive to the variegated and ever-changing play of light, continually elated at this spectacle of sky and ice and shadows.

The cold temperatures increased the difficulties of every aspect of his work. To guard against the condensation that developed on his cameras when they were carried from the outside into the ship's warmer interior, Hurley made a storage cupboard on deck, where they could be kept at a fairly constant temperature.

"Nevertheless," he wrote, "my apparatus needs attention every occasion it is taken out. Lubricating with petroleum etc., especially the cine. The film becoming extremely brittle."

The processing, too, was conducted under less than ideal conditions.

"Darkroom work rendered extremely difficult by the low temperatures it being –13 outside," he wrote towards the end of the winter. "The darkroom situated abaft the engine room is raised to above freezing point by a primus stove. . . . Washing [plates] is troublesome as the tank must be kept warm or the plates become an enclosure in an ice block. After several changes [of water] I place them in a rack in Sir E's Cabin — which is generally at an equable temperature. The Dry plates are all spotted & carefully indexed. Development is a source of annoyance to the fingers which split & crack around the nails in a painful manner."

Hurley aloft, Shackleton on deck

"Hurley was very busy with his camera and cinematograph machine, getting photos. He . . . fixed his machine on the extreme end of the top-gallant yard, to get panoramic views of the Pack."
(*Macklin, diary*)

Hurley with camera

Elsewhere he dryly notes "difficulty in obtaining sufficient water for washing operations." All water, of course, had to be melted from blocks of ice.

April, in Shackleton's words, "was not uneventful." Twice that month, the ice groaned around the ship, nipping her sides and causing the *Endurance* to vibrate slightly; it was the first palpable hint of the pack's deadly potential.

On the last day of the month, the ship's company were entertained by a rare spectacle. Shackleton and Worsley took a break from inspecting Lees's motor sledge and, inspired by some private whimsy, danced together in a stately waltz on the ice, while a member of the crew whistled "The Policeman's Holiday." Lees's record of this improbable event was perceptive.

"That is Sir Ernest all over," he wrote of the famous polar explorer's courtly gyrations. "He is always able to keep his troubles under and show a bold front. His unfailing cheeriness means a lot to a band of disappointed explorers like ourselves. In spite of his own great disappointment and we all know that is disasterous enough, he never appears to be anything but the acme of good humour and hopefulness. He is one of the greatest optimists living. . . . [H]e enters the lists every time with the spirit that every prize fighter enters the ring with."

In June began the darkest part of the year. Save for the moon and a couple of hours of dim twilight at noon, there was no light. The temperature had dropped to the minus twenties and leads of water that had been clear only the day before became encrusted with six inches of ice overnight.

During this darkening period of dead calm, on June 9, heavy pressure broke. Some 500 yards from the ship, colossal plates of ice screamed and groaned against each other, exploding now and then with the muffled boom of distant artillery. Guided by hand lanterns, several men went out to observe the pressure as it piled huge blocks of ice, each many tons in weight, one atop the other, to a height of fifteen feet. The

<u>Endurance</u> in the Ice, 4 April 1915
"During the night of the 3rd we heard the ice grinding to the eastward, and in the morning we saw that young ice was rafted 8 to 10 ft. high in places. This was the first murmur of the danger that was to reach menacing proportions in later months." (Shackleton, *South*)

roaring continued through June 12, but the weather thickened, making more excursions impossible.

By June 15, all was calm again, and a race between dog teams was planned for the following day. The rollicking Dog Derby was a much welcome diversion after the ominous bout of pressure. In the twilight, the track was lit with hurricane lamps, and Shackleton himself acted as starter. He had given all hands the day off, and several of the able seamen entered into the spirit of the day by appearing dressed as bookies, although, as Hurley remarked, "as they look a trifle 'disreputable,' their odds are not accepted." With a flutter of handkerchiefs and cheers of encouragement, the dogs were off. Wild's team won, having covered the 700 yards in two minutes and sixteen seconds.

Only days later, yet another holiday was festively observed. June 22, Midwinter's Day, was commemorated with a feast and after-dinner entertainment. Hurley erected a stage decorated with bunting and set up acetylene footlights. An overture, "Discord Fantasia in four flats," was performed by the Billabong Band, while James offered the most successful sketch of the evening, appearing as Herr Professor von Schopenbaum to give a Dissertation on The Calorie.

"Very witty & truly unintelligible," Worsley wrote appreciatively. After mid-

**Midwinter Dinner,
22 June 1915**

*"Dinner at 6-0 Roast Pork
stewed apples & preserves peas
with plum pudding."*
(McNish, diary)

night, the company sang "God Save the King" and wished one another well for the days ahead.

"From within the cosiness of the Ritz, it is hard to imagine we are drifting, frozen and solid in a sea of pack ice in the heart of the Weddell Sea," Hurley wrote. Yet, he added, "I often wonder what is to become of it all." His words imply that certain possibilities were not discussed, even as the creaking, booming sounds of distant pressure were carried through the crisp air to the stricken ship.

By the end of June, the *Endurance* had drifted more than 670 miles since her entrapment, and each mile brought her closer to the open water beyond the pack, and to the prospect of freedom. The hours of daylight were now increasing appreciably, and the men could look forward to seeing the sun again. Dog exercising became easier with the returning light, and concerts and lantern slide lectures continued as entertainment.

After several days of clear calm, a strong gale arose on July 12 and grew into a full-blown blizzard on July 13. The ship quivered as the pressure ground around her. Wild and Worsley were visiting with Shackleton in his cabin.

"The wind howled in the rigging," Worsley recalled, "and I couldn't help thinking that it was making just the sort of sound that you would expect a human being to utter if he were in fear of being murdered." In the lulls of the wind, the three men listened to the grinding of ice against the ship's sides. It was now that Shackleton shared what he had known for many months.

"The ship can't live in this, Skipper," he said, pausing in his restless march up and down the small cabin. "You had better make up your mind that it is only a matter of time. It may be a few months, and it may be only a question of weeks, or even days . . . but what the ice gets, the ice keeps."

Worsley reports that he received this news with despair and incredulity, and it is difficult to tell whether, in the few remaining months ahead, he regarded the loss of his ship as truly inevitable. He was, in his way, a more incurable optimist than Shackleton.

But Shackleton knew, and what Shackleton knew Wild took on faith. The men left their meeting and went back to the old routine, betraying nothing.

"It is bitterly cold and no one is allowed away from the ship," Hurley wrote the following day. "We are not anxious however. The alluring cosiness of the Ritz being too enticing." On the opposite side of the Ritz, however, McNish was writing in his diary from a very different perspective.

"We had a slight shock last night or this morning early," the old seaman wrote. "At least there was a noise under the bottom aft the same as if the ice had broken up

Crew of the <u>Endurance</u>

"The keel is jamed & there is no way in clearing it but at present everything is quiet & we are freezing in again but there is a lot of craks around the floe Hurley took a groupe of all hands on Wednesday."
(McNish, diary)

I jumped on deck but we could not find out what it was the Boss thinks it was a whale but I think different."

On July 21, amid heavy pressure, Shackleton ordered the decks cleared in the event the dogs had to be evacuated from the breaking ice; hourly watches were set throughout the night. The following day, Worsley rushed into the Ritz to announce that the ice had cracked some thirty yards ahead of them. All hands donned Burberrys and head gear and hurried outside. Some 300 yards off the port bow, colossal pressure was piling up massive blocks of ice as if they were sugar cubes. The sledges were brought off the floe, and Shackleton, Wild, and Worsley each took a four-hour watch during the night; Shackleton's daily sleep was now down to about three hours in the afternoon.

Over the ensuing days, emergency rations were stored with the sledges, ready for use, and on August 1, the dogs were hastily brought on board shortly before a wave of pressure caused blocks of ice to flatten the kennels and grind them to powder between the jaws of opening and closing floes. A large lump of ice that had become jammed under the rudder was maneuvered away, but damage had already been done.

As the gale raged, the *Endurance* was shaken like a toy by the pressure, knocked to her port side and nipped forward, backward, and side to side. Soundlessly she

At close of Winter. August 1, 1915

"Our position became extremely perilous, as huge blocks were rafting and tumbling over themselves in their apparent eagerness to hurl their force against our walls." (Hurley, diary)

New leads covered with ice flowers—early spring

"Took color camera to lead this morning amidst similar gorgeous conditions of yesterday & more glorified perhaps for a fine crop of ice flowers springing up on the lead & they, illumined by the morning sun, resembled a field of pink carnations." (Hurley, diary)

The Return of the Sun

"Extremely heavy precipitation of rime crystals during the night, our rigging being heavily encrusted, some of the ropes being over 3" in diameter, but the effect is beautiful." (Hurley, diary)

resisted, but when this onslaught ceased, a massive new pressure compressed her sides, causing her to strain and groan until her beams actually buckled.

"Everyone got our warm clothes put up in as small a bundle as possible," wrote McNish that night. "I have placed my Loved ones fotos inside Bible we got presented with from Queen Alexandra & put them in my bag."

Around the ship, blocks of ice caught between moving floes jumped like cherry-stones squeezed between a gigantic thumb and finger. The wind blew hard all night, then dropped the following day, when all became quiet, save for an occasional distant rumbling. Shackleton calculated that the gale had caused the ship to drift as much as thirty-seven miles north in the three days it had raged.

Throughout this ordeal, Lees, recovering from sciatica, had lain alone in Marston's bunk, to which he had been moved at his own request. From this deck cabin, he had listened to the rumbling and upheaval of the ice and the tramping of the watchman's feet overhead. While the ship rocked and trembled, he held his breath, waiting to see how she would settle. On August 9, he ventured outside for the first time in three weeks, thinner and greatly weakened.

Outside, an amazing sight awaited him: The *Endurance* lay in an entirely new landscape. All the old, familiar landmarks were gone or dislocated, and the ship appeared to have been forced forward a hundred yards through ice six feet thick.

"How this little ship survived amidst such a mighty upheaval is almost inconceivable," he wrote. "As it is she lies very much on her side with her rudder cracked & surrounded by great piles of ice blocks rising as high as her decks. We used to step

The pups (by Sally and Samson)

Left to right, Nell, Toby, Roger, and Nelson.

"In addition to their foster-father, Crean, the pups adopted Amundsen. They tyrannized over him most unmercifully. It was a common sight to see him, the biggest dog in the pack, sitting out in the cold with an air of philosophic resignation while a corpulent pup occupied the entrance to his dogloo."

(Shackleton, South)

out onto a comparatively level floe, now, on stepping outside, one finds oneself immediately in a labyrinth of ice blocks & gullies."

Yet the *Endurance* had survived, and the pressure had vanished. Gradually, the weather cleared, and as the winter drew to a close the sun tentatively returned, shining for several hours each day. Spirits rose as old routines were resumed. The greatest amusement was provided by Crean, who was undertaking to train the puppies he had nursed so tenderly. On their first day in harness his fat charges (now weighing some seventy pounds each) lay on their backs, waved their legs in the air, and squealed.

"Their howls and roars of terror resound for miles around," wrote Worsley, one of the many bystanders entertained by the spectacle. "They pursue a devious and uncertain course. . . . [T]hough each pup possesses the voice of Jeremiah, his paunch is the paunch of Falstaff, and they flounder puff and pant along through the snow until to their joy they are headed for the ship and for a few minutes drag the hated sledge almost as fast as a dog team. Crean expects in two more lessons to teach them to drag a sledge unaided by an old leader. They will then be formally promoted from 'Purps' to 'Dags.'"

Taking the dogs out for exercise

After severe ice pressure forced the evacuation of the dogs from the dogloos to the ship, they were disembarked every other day for exercise.

The rest of August passed without incident. Glorious sunrises tinted the ice pink, and delicate ice formations that formed on new leads of water resembled fields of carnations. On the night of August 27, with the temperature at −24°, Hurley set up twenty flashes behind hummocks of ice around the stricken *Endurance*.

"Half blinded after the successive flashes," he recorded, "I lost my bearings amidst hummocks, bumping shins against projecting ice points & stumbling into deep snow drifts." But the image he secured was haunting: the rime-crusted *Endurance* breasting the ice, a spectral ship, both gallant and vulnerable.

Spring was on the way. The men began to speculate whether on breaking out they would immediately return to Vahsel Bay and embark upon the transcontinental crossing or would return to civilization first for provisions. Bets were placed on

Harnessing the dogs

"The harness is similar to that used by Amundsen, consisting of a padded collar attached to traces, which fit over the dog & is secured by a belly band."
(Hurley, diary)

Dog team being exercised over pressure ice.
"A good leader will ferret out the best track through rough or broken country, will not allow fights in the team, or indulge in any capricious antics. . . . A team of nine dogs can haul about 1,000 lbs."
(Hurley, diary)

The dog teams

"One team appears to suffer from heart disease, their owner evidently expecting the whole creation to hold their breath as they pass by. A vulgar person . . . had the indescribable effrontery to let go his horrid war cry whilst riding on the imposing conveyance drawn by these dignified but nervous creatures, and was reproved by their indignant owner pointing out to the Vulgar Person into what terror his voice had thrown the beautiful but highly strung and delicate doggies." (Worsley, diary)

The <u>Endurance</u> at Night

August 27, 1915: "During night take flashlight of ship beset by pressure. This necessitated some 20 flashes, one behind each salient pressure hummock, no less than 10 of the flashes being required to satisfactorily illuminate the ship herself. Half blinded after the successive flashes, I lost my bearings amidst hummocks, bumping shins against projecting ice points & stumbling into deep snow drifts." (Hurley, diary)

The floe cracking up, 29 Sept. 1915

"My Birthday & I sincerely hope to spend my next one at Home there is a fine breeze a Southerly wind at present & there is a crack in the floe about 10 yards ahead of the ship if the wind holds in this direction for a while it will open the ice up."
(*McNish, diary*)

the "breakout" date: McIlroy hazarded November 3; Lees, ever pessimistic, thought it unlikely to occur before mid-February; Shackleton said he believed it would be October 2.

The pressure returned on the night of August 26. For several days it presented no immediate danger, but in the early hours of September 2, it took hold of the *Endurance* with a vengeance.

"On the night of 2nd September, I had one of the most startling moments of my life," Bakewell recalled. "I was lying in my bunk, when . . . the ship literally jumped into the air and settled on its beam." The iron plates in the engine room buckled, door frames were distorted, beams bulged as if they would splinter. The *Endurance* struggled and groaned as if in mortal pain.

"There were times when we thought it was not possible the ship would stand it," wrote McNish. He had watched the three-foot-square iron plates bulge up one and a half inches. But the pressure passed, and a week later McNish was busy building a wheelhouse that would protect the steersman from the elements, once they were under way again. Meanwhile, Shackleton had privately calculated that they were 250 miles away from the nearest known land, and more than 500 from the nearest outpost of civilization.

September unfolded without further crises, although the roar of distant pressure was seldom absent, and the floes around the ship were in constant movement. The men played football on the shifting floes, exercised the dogs, and hunted for seals, which were returning with the promise of spring. A light snowfall one night left the ship shimmering as if tinselled, and the ice sparkling as though covered with diamonds.

On the afternoon of September 20, the most severe bout of pressure encountered so far shook the *Endurance* from mast to keel, so that it seemed her sides would have to collapse. But an hour later, the pressure subsided.

It was October 1915. On the third day of the month, heavy pressure broke ten yards from the ship. The *Endurance* was by now as frozen onto the blocks of ice beneath her, in Lees's words, "as any rock in a glacier." During a brief opening of the ice around the ship, the men had gazed down into the open water by her side and seen, spotlit by the penetrating sun, great azure-blue conglomerates of ice lying as much as forty feet below the surface. Frost smoke rose from out of the open leads, red tinged at sunrise so that the ice seemed at times to be aflame.

High temperatures—up to 29°—on the 10th produced a general, mushy thaw. The men started packing up the Ritz, and on the 13th returned to their original quarters. The following night, the floe on which the *Endurance* was lodged suddenly split; the ice slithered out from under the ship, and she floated on an even keel, in clear water for the first time in nine months. Impelled by the gale that had arisen, she swung in the narrow lead, and actually drove 100 yards ahead. Then the ice closed on her, and she was fast again.

An hour later

Over the following days, while the pack was still loose, Shackleton had the sails set, and an effort was made to force the ship ahead, but with no success. Shortly after tea on the 16th, after several loud bumps against her sides, the *Endurance* began to rise above the ice, squeezed up between the floes—then was abruptly thrown on her port side, listing some 30 degrees. Kennels, dogs, sledges, stores were all thrown across the deck into a tangled, howling heap. Then, around nine in the evening, the pressure subsided, and the ship returned to an even keel.

On the 19th, Shackleton had the boilers filled and fires banked in readiness, and ice debris was cleared from around the rudder and the ship. McNish was commissioned to build a small punt, with a view to navigating the leads and channels. Light snow fell off and on throughout the day, and in the evening a killer whale appeared in the tiny pool around the ship, his huge body seen plainly through the calm, clear water as he cruised, leisurely, up and down beside the stricken ship.

In the following days, the roar of pressure was continually in the men's ears, likened, by James, to the sound of London traffic when one is sitting quietly in a park. Sea watches were resumed, while the ice floes ground around the ship. The *Endurance* was now shaken and beaten constantly, but the men had become so accustomed to the disruptions that they were indifferent to all but the most violent upheavals.

"Personally," wrote Worsley, "I've got tired of alarm against which we can do absolutely nothing." The dogs, restless from lack of exercise, howled and whimpered as the ominous sounds arose from the ice.

"The ice is opening up a bit, thank goodness," Lees wrote on the 23rd. "Things look a little more hopeful." After a dinner of salt beef, carrots, mashed potatoes, and Banbury tarts, the traditional Saturday night toast was drunk to "Sweethearts and Wives." There was now as much as twenty-two hours of daylight each day.

On Sunday, October 24, the men watched the pressure move across the ice throughout the otherwise uneventful day. In the evening after dinner, Lees had just put "The Wearing of the Green" on the gramophone when a terrific crash shook the ship like an earthquake, causing her to shiver and list over about 8 degrees to starboard. The men finished listening to the tune, then went up on deck, according to Lees, "to see if anything unusual had occurred." They found Shackleton on the ice with a grave face, examining the ship's sternpost. Caught between three separate pressure ridges across her bow and both sides, the *Endurance* had been twisted and bent by their onslaught. The sternpost had been almost wrenched out and was leaking dangerously.

Immediately, Shackleton gave the order to raise steam for the engine room pumps. With water rising rapidly, the engineers, Rickinson and Kerr, desperately piled on fuel—coal, blubber, wood—racing to raise steam before the rising water could put the fires out. Within two hours they had the pump working, but they soon saw that

The <u>Endurance</u> keeling over

"Suddenly the floe on the port side cracked and huge pieces of ice shot up from under the port bilge. Within a few seconds the ship heeled over until she had a list of thirty degrees to port."

(Shackleton, South)

it could not cope with the inrush of water. Hudson, Greenstreet, and Worsley disappeared into the bunkers, where the coal was stored, to clear the bilge pump, which had been jammed with ice all winter. Digging through the coal in the darkness, now underneath icy black water, they succeeded by early morning in clearing the pump with a blowtorch, and it was worked in shifts throughout the night.

On the floes, the men took turns away from the pumps to dig desperate, ineffectual trenches around their dying ship. Inside, the sound of running water and the clickety-clack of the pumps rose above the creaking of the ship's tortured timbers. Down in the engine room, Chippy McNish was working with fierce concentration, building a cofferdam across the stern to contain the leak. Crouched in the water that rose at times to his waist, he toiled unremittingly through the night. Meanwhile, all other hands were feverishly gathering together stores, clothing, sledging gear, and dog food in preparation for disembarking onto the ice. Worsley went through the ship's library, tearing maps, charts, even photographs of possible landfalls out of the books they would have to leave behind. Marston, Lees, and James worked in the after hold removing supplies while the sound of rushing water resounded beneath them and the ship's beams cracked and exploded like pistol shots overhead. On the follow-

ing morning, Hurley visited McNish, who had labored without rest on the coffer-dam, and found that the leak had been checked.

"The water is level with the engine room floor but it is being easily kept under," he wrote. "We still hope to bring our staunch little craft through."

It was a cloudy, misty day. Pressure could be seen and heard all around, raising the ice to unimagined heights, but the ship herself was quiet. McNish still toiled on in the engine room, filling with concrete the space between the two bulkheads he had built and caulking them with strips of torn blankets.

"Things look a bit more promising now," wrote Wordie later in the day. "The sun is shining for one thing, and we are hoping the cofferdam is a success." From four in the afternoon until midnight, the pumps were worked continuously, until the incoming water was under control. All stores were shifted from the stern, so as to raise it above the water when the ice opened and allowed the ship to float again. Only the bilge pump was worked throughout the night, and the exhausted men snatched minutes of sleep despite the faint whispers of distress that arose from the ship. Chippy McNish was still below working on the cofferdam.

The 26th dawned clear, save for gentle, fleecy clouds, and full of sunshine that glinted with sparkling beauty off the ice. With the roar of pressure in his ears, Shackleton was struck by the surreal incongruity between the serene beauty of the day and the death throes of his ship; from the bridge, he had seen how the pressure was actually bending her like a bow, and it had seemed to Worsley that she was gasping to draw breath. She was leaking badly again, and the exhausted men worked the pumps in shifts—fifteen minutes on, fifteen minutes off—half asleep on their feet. At nine in the evening, Shackleton ordered the lifeboats and sledges lowered to a stable floe. The leak slowed, stanched to some degree by movement of the ice.

"All hope is not given up yet for saving the ship," wrote Hurley. Nevertheless, he took the precaution of packing his photo album in waterproof cloth—"it being the only record of my work I shall be able to take, should we be compelled to take to the floe." The *Endurance* had quieted, but that evening an unsettling incident occurred while several sailors were on deck. A band of eight emperor penguins solemnly approached, an unusually large number to be travelling together. Intently regarding the ship for some moments, they threw back their heads and emitted an eerie, soulful cry.

"I myself must confess that I have never, either before or since, heard them make any sound similar to the sinister wailings they moaned that day," wrote Worsley. "I cannot explain the incident." It was as if the emperors had sung the ship's dirge. McLeod, the most superstitious of the seamen, turned to Macklin and said, "Do you hear that? We'll none of us get back to our homes again."

They continued to work the pumps throughout the night and morning. October 27 dawned clear and bright, but with a temperature of –8.5°. The ice had not ceased to roar, but the men were now too tired to notice. The pumps were being worked faster and faster, and someone was actually singing a chanty to their beat. The pressure increased throughout the day and at 4 p.m., reached its height. With a blow, the ship was knocked stern up, while a moving floe ripped away her rudder and sternpost; then the floe relaxed, and the beaten *Endurance* sank a little in the water. The decks began to break upward, and as the keel was ripped out, the water poured in.

It was all up. At 5 p.m., Shackleton gave the order to abandon ship. The dogs were evacuated down canvas chutes, and the supplies that had been readied were lowered to the ice. Shackleton, standing on the quivering deck, looked down the engine-room skylight to see the engines dropping sideways as the stays and plates gave way.

"Everything has come too quickly to make us pause to regret," wrote Wordie. "That will come in the future." The men were numbed by fatigue and the suddenness with which the end had come. None of the diaries evinces much concern for personal safety; all emotion was expended on the death of the ship. From her first entrance into the pack, they had cheered her fighting spirit; "noble," "gallant," "brave," "our stout little ship"—these had been the proud words with which they had characterized her. It was her maiden journey—she was, in Hurley's words, "a bride of the sea."

"It is hard to write what I feel," wrote Shackleton. "To a sailor his ship is more than a floating home. . . . Now, straining and groaning, her timbers cracking and her wounds gaping, she is slowly giving up her sentient life at the very outset of her career."

Before departing for good, Hurley had taken one last look around their old quarters in the Ritz, already a foot deep in water. The sound of beams splintering in the darkness was alarming, and he abruptly left. But of all sights and sounds, it was the clock still ticking comfortably in the cozy wardroom as the water rose that perhaps most unnerved him.

Shackleton was the last to leave. He hoisted the blue ensign, and the men on the ice gave three hearty cheers. By a cruel accident, the ship's emergency light had switched on, and as its circuit was intermittently broken, the *Endurance* seemed to all hands to bid them a final, sad, flickering farewell.

The wreck of the <u>Endurance</u>

"The floes are in a state of agitation throughout the day, and in consequence, I had the cinema trained on the ship the whole time. I secured the unique film of the mast collapsing. Toward evening, as though conscious of having achieved its purpose, the floes were quiescent again." (Hurley, diary)

The wreck of the <u>Endurance</u>

"Awful calamity that has overtaken the ship that has been our home for over 12 months. . . . We are homeless & adrift on the sea ice." (Hurley, diary)

Patience Camp

For the Crew of the <u>Endurance</u> From Alexandra, May 31, 1914
May the Lord help you to do your duty & guide you through all dangers by land and sea.
"May you see the Works of the Lord & all His wonders in the Deep."

—INSCRIPTION IN SHIP BIBLE
PRESENTED BY QUEEN ALEXANDRA

"Assemble on floe: Boss explains situation and we turn in," wrote Wordie. They had set up camp on what appeared to be a stable floe only some 100 yards from their shattered ship. As far as could be seen in every direction around them, the ice rose in contorted, colossal fragments. The temperature had fallen to −15°. They were 350 miles from the nearest land.

Each man was issued a sleeping bag and assigned to one of five tents.

"There was only 18 skin bags & we cast lots for them," wrote McNish. "I was lucky for the first time in my life for I drew one." By some piece of subterfuge that did not escape the sailors, most of the officers happened to draw the less desirable Jaeger wool bags.

"There was some crooked work in the drawing," Able Seaman Bakewell recorded, "as Sir Ernest, Mr. Wild . . . Captain Worsley and some of the other officers all drew wool bags. The fine warm fur bags all went to the men under them."

Lying on groundsheets that were not waterproof, the men listened to the grinding and booming of the floes, like distant thunder, travelling through the ice directly under their heads, the sound now unmuffled by their ship's stout wooden walls. Their linen tents were so thin that the moon could be seen through them. Three times in the night, the floe on which they were camped cracked beneath them. Three times they had to pick up tent, sleeping bag, and groundsheet and pitch them all again.

"A terrible night," wrote James, "with the ship outline dark against the sky & the noise of the pressure against her . . . seeming like the cries of a living creature."

Shackleton himself did not return to his tent, but paced the ice, listening to the pressure and staring at the light in his ship. "Like a lamp in a cottage window, it braved the night," he wrote, "until in the early morning the *Endurance* received

Shackleton's caption for this photograph in South *was "The End."*

93

Dump Camp. The morning after the disaster to the ship

"A terrible night with the ship outline dark against the sky & the noise of the pressure against her . . . like the cries of a living creature" (James, diary). *The men passed the first three nights on the ice here before attempting to march to land 364 miles away.*

a particularly violent squeeze. There was a sound of rending beams and the light disappeared."

In the chill dawn, Shackleton was joined by Hurley and Wild in salvaging tins of petrol from the wreck. Erecting a makeshift galley, they prepared warm milk and took it to the men in their tents, "surprised and a trifle chagrined," as Shackleton recorded dryly, "at the matter-of-fact manner in which some of the men accepted this contribution to their comfort. They did not quite understand what work we had done for them in the early dawn, and I heard Wild say, 'If any of you gentlemen would like your boots cleaned just put them outside!'"

After breakfast, Shackleton again summoned the men and informed them that in a few days they would begin a march towards Snow Hill or Robertson Island, some 200 miles to the northwest.

"As always with him what had happened had happened," Macklin wrote. "It was in the past and he looked to the future. . . . [W]ithout emotion, melodrama or excitement [he] said 'ship and stores have gone—so now we'll go home.'"

The planned march required the men to drag with them basic supplies as well as two of the three lifeboats. Every hand had been issued new winter gear and a pound of tobacco. Beyond this, each was limited to two pounds of personal possessions. A few exceptions were made. Shackleton allowed Hussey to take his banjo, on the premise that it would supply the men with "vital mental tonic."

By way of example, before the assembled men, Shackleton discarded a handful of gold sovereigns and his gold watch on the ice, followed by his silver brushes and dressing cases. He then took the Bible that had been presented to the ship before departure by Queen Alexandra. Ripping out the flyleaf and a few other pages, he lay the Bible on the ice. The pages he retained were those of the Twenty-third Psalm and these verses from Job:

> Out of whose womb came the ice?
> And the hoary frost of Heaven, who hath gendered it?
> The waters are hid as with a stone
> And the face of the deep is frozen.

A pile of discarded dress uniforms, scientific equipment, books, watches, cooking utensils, ropes, tools, flags, sextants, chronometers, diaries, and blankets grew as the men dumped all nonessential personal effects. McNish was busy fitting the boats to sledges, while others sorted rations, stored their gear, and sewed pockets on their clothing for precious possessions like spoons, knives, toilet paper, and toothbrushes.

There were no disturbances over the next two nights, and on October 30 the men awoke to a raw, snowy morning. Everything was ready for the start of the march, and at 1:15 p.m. a "pioneering party" consisting of Shackleton, Hudson, Hurley, and Wordie got under way. Shackleton shouted, "Now we start for Robertson Island, boys!" and everyone cheered. The job of this advance guard was to attempt to break down the hummocks, ice blocks, and pressure ridges over which the boats and dogsledges would travel.

At 2:55 p.m., Crean shot three of his puppies and Mrs. Chippy, who had come to be known as the ship's mascot. It was left to Macklin to put down his dog Sirius, who had never been broken to harness. Sirius, ever friendly, jumped up to lick Macklin's hand, which was shaking so much that he required two shots to finish the job. The sound of the shots ringing out over the ice cast a pall over an already gloomy day.

At 3 p.m., the rest of the procession set out. From the pathfinding party at the head to the fifteen man-hauling the large lifeboat in the rear, the unwieldy column stretched for as much as a mile. Seven dog teams relayed back and forth with smaller loads.

At 6 p.m., the party halted for the night. They had travelled just under a mile.

"A wretched day," Lees wrote the following morning. "Snowing hard with a very high temperature & everything wet." Owing to the snow, they did not set out until the afternoon; after they had travelled only half a mile, the weather thickened, and Shackleton called a halt. On the third day, November 1, sinking at times up to their hips in the wet snow, they covered a quarter of a mile before calling it quits.

"The condition of the surface is atrocious," wrote Hurley. "There appears scarcely a square yard of smooth surface which is covered by a labyrinth of hummocks & ridges." After a conference with his ad hoc advisory committee, consisting of Wild,

Hauling the <u>James Caird</u>

"We all followed with the heavier boat on the composite sledge. It was terrific work to keep it going. We all did our best but were practically exhausted by the time we reached the new camp, No. 4, barely ¾ miles away" (Lees, diary). Loaded, the boats weighed as much as a ton each.

A distant view of the camp

When the march was abandoned, Ocean Camp was established on a solid floe roughly a mile and a half from the wreck of the Endurance, *which was still visible in the distance; the tip of its broken mast and funnel can just be seen over the horizon to the left of the photograph.*

Worsley, and Hurley, Shackleton acknowledged that further efforts were futile. He announced that they would pitch a new camp and await the breakup of the ice, which would allow them to take the boats into open water. His hope was that the drift of the pack would carry them northwest to within striking distance of Paulet Island, nearly 400 miles distant. Nordenskjöld's Swedish expedition had built a hut there in 1902, and Shackleton knew it to be stocked with emergency supplies; he himself had helped provision the relief operation for the expedition twelve years earlier. From here, a small overland party would continue west to Graham Land, and make its way to Wilhelmina Bay, where they could expect to meet up with whaling vessels. Meanwhile, the new camp, established on a sturdy floe some twenty feet thick only a mile and a half from the wreck of the *Endurance*, was christened Ocean Camp.

Throughout the ensuing days, salvage teams ferried back and forth between

"Dump Camp," the site where the *Endurance* had been abandoned, and their new quarters. Many objects removed from the ship during the disaster had sunk into the snow and become embedded in the ice. Nonetheless, much was retrieved, including part of the *Encyclopaedia Britannica*. The entire wheelhouse, now under three feet of water, was removed from the ship's deck and put to use as a storehouse. McNish hacked an opening through the deck above the old Ritz, disgorging various cases of food, some more useful than others: Containers of sugar and flour floated out to loud cheers, while the appearances of walnuts, onions, and soda carbonate were met with groans.

It was during this time of precarious digging in the bowels of the wrecked ship that Hurley determined to rescue his negatives.

"During the day," he wrote, "I hacked through the thick walls of the refrigerator to retrieve the negatives stored therein. They were located beneath four feet of mushy ice & by stripping to the waist & diving under I hauled them out. Fortunately they are soldered up in double tin linings, so I am hopeful they may not have suffered by their submersion."

As the new plan called for eventual recourse to the boats, the weight of personal possessions allowed to each man was still strictly limited. But when Hurley returned with his precious negatives, Shackleton relented.

"I spend the day with Sir Ernest selecting the finest of my negatives from the year's collection," Hurley wrote on November 9. He resoldered 120 and dumped

The wreck
"The wardroom is a pile of broken timber, while as to the forehold I did not dare go in lest I should not get out again. . . . It was a sad sight to see the old familiar places broken up."
(*Macklin, diary*)

about 400. "This unfortunate reduction is essential, as a drastic cutting down in weight must be effected owing to the very limited space that will be at disposal in boat transport." The selected negatives included twenty Paget color as well as 100 whole and half glass plates. He also retrieved an album of already developed prints.

"Mind you put your old diary in my bag as it has been kept rather more regularly than mine, I believe," Shackleton had said to Lees as they abandoned ship. At the back of his mind were the book and story rights he had sold in advance to finance the expedition. Hurley's photographs would be similarly valuable.

Ocean Camp

Lumber salvaged from the Endurance, *foreground, is used to build the new galley. "Half the members went off with dog sledges to the ship & all day long relays of wood, ropes & a few odd provisions were arriving at the camp." (Lees, diary)*

Three tons of salvaged provisions were eventually carried back to Ocean Camp on dogsledges and stored in the former wheelhouse, now nicknamed "the rabbit hutch." The new camp gained shape. In the center stood the galley, built of sails and spars and containing a stove that Hurley had constructed with a chisel from the ship's ash chute. Nearby stood the line of three domed and two pole tents, close to which the dogs were pegged out in their teams. A platform of deck planking and spars served as a lookout, over which were flown the flags of the King and the Royal Clyde Yacht Club.

A routine was established. At 8:30 a.m., breakfast was served consisting of fried seal, lumps of baked dough called "bannocks," and tea. Each tent appointed a mess-man, whose job was to bring meals from the galley to the tent. After breakfast, parties went out scouting for seals or did chores around the camp until lunch, at 1 p.m. Afternoons were spent as one chose, generally reading, darning, or walking. At 5:30,

Ocean Camp

Shackleton and Wild stand in the left foreground; Bakewell's Winchester .30-.30 carbine (a "saddle gun" purchased in Montana) is propped beside Wild. The wood-slatted rear of the storehouse is beyond to the right. Hurley's camera equipment is in cases to the left of Shackleton. The sailors are mostly to the right.

"It is beyond conception, even to us, that we are dwelling on a colossal ice raft, with but five feet of ice separating us from 2,000 fathoms of ocean, & drifting along under the caprices of wind & tides, to heaven knows where."
(*Hurley, diary*)

penguin stew ("hoosh") was served with cocoa, and immediately afterward the crew settled into their sleeping bags. Hour watches were set throughout the night, to guard against dogs "coming adrift" or to warn the camp of a sudden breakup of the floe.

The sledging rations originally intended for the continental crossing had been among the first articles evacuated from the ship before the breakup, and were now scrupulously reserved for the boat journey, which was projected to be only a month or two away. Estimates of how long the rest of the salvaged food could last varied from personality to personality: According to Hurley, there was "now sufficient food in the camp augmented with seals and penguins, to last the party nine months." Lees's practiced calculations, nearer the mark, did not extend much beyond 100 days. Shackleton allocated a pound of food per man per day, a diet that was uncomfortably frugal, but far from starvation. The men's main criticism at this point concerned the monotony of the fare.

Shackleton's tent assignments were characteristically astute.

"He collected with him the ones he thought wouldn't mix with the others. . . . They were not so easy to get on with, the ones he had in his tent with him—they were quite a mixed bag," according to Greenstreet. With Shackleton in tent No. 1 were Hurley, Hudson, and James; James had proved to be fair game for teasing and baiting, and his inclusion was for his own good. Hurley was included because his vanity was flattered by being with "the Boss." Shackleton was very wary of Hurley, whose undoubted competence and somewhat glamorous professional background had won him a following early in the expedition. In terms of mental and physical toughness, Hurley was up with Wild and Crean—but he lacked their unquestionable loyalty. Consequently, Shackleton took pains to "consult" with Hurley, and to include him in all conferences of any importance.

Wild, Wordie, McIlroy, and McNish shared tent No. 2, Shackleton placing the dour carpenter squarely in the midst of men he regarded as "solid," under Wild's eye. Tent No. 3, a large domed construction, held the eight men from the fo'c'sle, How, Bakewell, McCarthy, McLeod, Vincent, Holness, Stephenson, and Green—who would have expected to remain together. Crean had charge of the generally unproblematic tent No. 4 with Hussey, Marston, and Cheetham; and Worsley was in charge of tent No. 5, the other large tent, with Greenstreet, Lees, Clark, Kerr, Rickinson, Macklin, and Blackborow.

The days passed in largely unrelieved but not altogether unpleasant idleness. Apart from speculations on the progress of the war in Europe, the most impassioned conversations concerned the weather, the wind, and the rate of ice drift.

"The Blizard still continues but we all hope it lasts for a month as we have done 16 miles NW since our last observation," McNish wrote on November 6, the day of their first heavy snowstorm on the ice. The direction as well as rate of the drift was all-important. Ideally, the generally prevailing northwest current would take them to the long arm of the Palmer Peninsula, in the vicinity of Snow Hill, Robertson, or Paulet Islands; on the other hand, there was a danger that drift might stray to the northeast or east—away from land. It was also possible, of course, that the pack would stall, in which case they would face another winter on the ice.

In mid-November, the weather turned unusually mild, with temperatures in the upper 20s and even 30s. Although the warmth was welcomed as a sign of the impending breakup of the pack, living conditions in general became less comfortable. The camp was mired in slush, through which the men slogged, sometimes falling through rotten snow into hidden pools of water. Inside their tents, the temperature could rise to as much as 70°, now considered oppressively hot. All the tents were supplied with makeshift wooden floors, built of salvaged dog kennel and ship timber, but even these could not keep their sleeping bags entirely above the pools of water. At night, temperatures fell to zero, cold enough for the men's breath to precipitate as a light snow powder in the tents.

Inside, the men lay head to toe, like sardines in a tin, with no room to turn and nowhere to tread when they went out or came in. Inevitably, minor tensions were exacerbated.

"Tent walls are very thin," Lees wrote, "thinner than this paper, and they have ears on both sides—inside & outside and many are the scrappy bits one hears which one 'didn't ought' to hear." The role Lees himself came to play in the group was both

Ocean Camp

Shackleton, Wild, and an unidentified member of the crew stand right to left. This is one of the last photographs Hurley took with his professional equipment. It was taken sometime between November 9, when the sailors erected the lookout tower, seen with ship's burgee flying beneath the king's flag, and November 22, when Hurley soldered his camera lenses and negatives in hermetically sealed double tin cannisters. He also soldered his album of developed prints in a brass case. After that, all his photographs were taken with his Vest Pocket Kodak and three rolls of film.

Ocean Camp

The three lifeboats on sledge runners can be seen in the background.

fascinating and pathetic. In addition to his many other irritating traits, he was a snorer, and in early November he reported to his diary that "there is a movement on foot to eject me from the 8 man pole tent & make me sleep in the rabbit hutch." This campaign was successful, and shortly afterward Lees busily put the finishing touches to the sleeping accommodations in the storeroom.

"Sounds of bitter sobs and lamentations are heard this evening from No. 5 tent at the loss of their dearly beloved 'Colonel' who has removed himself for a season to sleep in his store in the old wheelhouse," Worsley wrote facetiously. Given Shackleton's almost obsessive care to keep his group together, physically and morally, it is striking that he allowed Lees to go off, or be driven off, in this manner. Yet there were clear reasons why he would have wanted Lees neutralized.

"A human being's normal diet should contain the three main constituents of food, protein, fat and carbo-hydrates in the proportion of 1–1–2½ respectively whatever the actual weights," Lees recorded in his diary, in a typical entry. "I.e. the carbo-hydrates (farinaceous foods and sugar) should be more than double the other two. . . . As it is, our flour will only last out for another ten weeks at the most," and so on, and on. The sight of Lees's nakedly anxious face, his incessant fussy inventory-taking and worried pronouncements of shortages must have driven Shackleton wild.

It did not help matters that Lees's observations were entirely correct. But Lees does not appear to have grasped the single salient fact of the crew's predicament—that by all rational calculations their situation was not merely desperate but impossible. Any strategy for survival, therefore, could not completely defer to reality; Shackleton's tactics always involved a dangerous gamble of morale against practical necessity. The last thing he needed was for the men to hear Lees's grim invocations of the laws of science and reason. Hence, a move to ostracize Lees, or undermine his credibility, could only have been welcomed by Shackleton.

On the other hand, certain practical measures could be taken, such as the preparation of the boats for their inevitable journey.

"I have been busy since Saturday finishing the sledge for the boat," wrote McNish on November 16, "& now I am building the boat up 1 foot higher & decking her in half way making her fit to carry the whole party in case we have to make a longer journey than we intisipate at present." The work was done with his only surviving tools—a saw, hammer, chisel, and adze. Less than two weeks later, he had finished all three boats, but was still tinkering.

"I have started to raise the *Dudley Docker* a strake higher at my leisure," he wrote. "It is pass time for me & it makes the boat carry more & more seaworthy." Everyone who stopped by was impressed by his work. In mid-December McNish was still tinkering with the boats. It was, as he said, "pass time." The particular object of his

"*The Wreckage Lies Around in Dismal Confusion. Wild taking a last look at the ship before she sank.*" (*Shackleton*, South) *Probably taken on November 14, 1915, when Wild and Hurley walked from Ocean Camp to take a look at the wreck, only seven days before she sank for good.*

care was the twenty-two-foot-long whaler, christened the *James Caird* after the expedition's principal benefactor. The boat had been commissioned by Worsley and built in a Thames dockyard according to his specifications.

"Her planking was Baltic pine, keel & timbers American elm & stem & sternpost English oak," according to Worsley. One of McNish's refinements was to put chafing battens on her bow, as he said, "to keep the young ice from cutting through as she is built of white pine which wont last long in ice." In lieu of the usual caulking materials—oakum and pitch—McNish had filled the seams with lamp wick and sealed them over with Marston's oil paints. The nails he used had been extracted from salvaged timber of the *Endurance*.

The landscape around them had subtly changed with the thaw. The convoluted ice fields had softened and were threaded with small, broken leads of water. The days were very long, with the sun rising at 3 a.m. and setting at 9 p.m. The crew passed the time by hunting seals amid the slush, playing cards, and arguing over articles in the *Encyclopaedia Britannica*. In tent No. 5, Clark read aloud from *Science from an Easy Chair*. Singsongs were still held in the evenings. Marston resoled everyone's boots, and Hurley was absorbed with improvising crampons for the march to the west from Snow Hill Island.

On the evening of November 21, shortly after the dogs had been fed, as the company read and chatted quietly in their tents, they heard Shackleton call out, "She's going." Hurrying outside to the lookout platform and other points of vantage, the men looked out to see the last moments of the *Endurance*. Her stern rising high in the air, she went down bows first in one quick dive.

"There was a queer silence over the camp," according to Bakewell. "As for me, there was an odd lump in my throat and I found it hard to swallow. . . . We were now very lonely."

"She's gone, boys," Shackleton said quietly from the lookout post. In his own diary he wrote, "At 5 p.m. she went down by the head: the stern the cause of all the trouble was the last to go under water. I cannot write about it."

As the thaw continued, leads of open water increased, making the still occasional salvage trips to Dump Camp and hunting excursions increasingly dangerous. It was with great difficulty that the dog teams negotiated paths through the ever-changing maze of open lanes to collect seals killed earlier by scouting hunters. The floe on which they were encamped had rotated as much as 15 degrees to the east in the loosening ice. Yet the pack as a whole showed no signs of breaking up.

"Really Sir Ernest does not at all ignore the possibility of having to remain on the floe until it reaches the vicinity of the South Orkneys," Lees reported. "But he does not like it to be discussed for fear of creating a feeling of despondency, especially among the sailors."

Old landmarks drifted regally across the waterlogged, slurry landscape. The crew's old friend the Rampert Berg was now a mere five miles distant and appeared to be dark blue, a sign that it might be floating in open water. Thick mist sometimes obscured the landscape; wet snow fell, and once actual rain. In late November, a blue sky gave way to showers of hail that fell on the tents with a sound that reminded Wordie of heavy rain on trees. They were drifting northwest at a rate of a little more than two miles a day.

December was not an easy month for Shackleton. Towards the end of November, he had come down with an attack of sciatica, which worsened over the following days, until he was unable to leave his sleeping bag without assistance; it could not have been helped by his lying in a wool bag on waterlogged timber. Worse, his confinement removed him somewhat from the goings-on in camp. James, who shared

Shackleton's tent, noted that "he was constantly on the watch for any break in morale, or any discontent, so that he could deal with it at once." Above all else, Shackleton feared losing his grip on his men. The period of illness made him anxious and restive, and when he finally recovered, some two weeks later, he emerged from his tent not altogether in the best of spirits. "Boss hauls cook over the coals for making doughy bannocks," Hurley recorded on Shackleton's first day up and about. The men, too, were restless, the sailors in particular showing worrisome signs of disaffection.

The entire company monitored the drift of their floe more intently than ever.

"Once across the Antarctic circle (66.31) it will seem as if we are practically half way home again," Lees noted on December 12. "And it is just possible that with favouring winds we may cross the circle before the new year." Only a few days later, a strong blizzard arising from the south promised to speed them over the magic line even sooner than anticipated; but on December 18, the wind swung around from the northeast, driving them back the way they had come. More disconcerting was the fact that their drift fluctuated between northwest and a subtle veer to the east, away from land. Shackleton discussed with Wild and Hurley the possibility of making another attempt to march to land, partly to forestall the ominous hint of an eastward drift; partly because, as Wild agreed, "a spell of hard work would do everybody good." On the 20th, the three men set out to scout the conditions.

"Found the surface & conditions good, there being about 75% of splendid going," Hurley reported optimistically. Shackleton broke the news to the rest of the company that they would be on the march again on December 23, the day after Mid-

**Galley on Ice; Orde-Lees
and Green the Cook**

*Their faces black with smoke
from the blubber stove, Lees and
Green prepare a meal in the
makeshift galley during the ill-
fated march from Ocean Camp
to Patience Camp.*

summer's Day, which was to be celebrated as Christmas. The announcement of this
second march came as an unwelcome shock to many. "As far as I have seen the going
will be awful," wrote Greenstreet. "Everything being in a state of softness far worse
than when we left the ship, and in my opinion it would be a measure to be taken only
as a last resort and I sincerely hope he will give up the idea directly. There have been
great arguments about the matter in our tent."

Despite the grand "blowout" feast for "Christmas," the breaking of camp on the
early morning of the 23rd was not accomplished in universally high spirits. Shackleton had determined that they should travel at night, when the surface of the ice was
hardest, and consequently the men were awakened at three in the morning on a
foggy, dreary day. The abortive first march had been undertaken with genuine optimism. On the second march, many set out in resigned, halfhearted obedience.

Eighteen men straining in harness relayed two of the boats ahead over the now
precarious ice; then all hands returned to pack up the remaining supplies. Tents, galley, stores, sledges were dragged as far as the boats, where a new camp was pitched;
the third boat was left behind at Ocean Camp. At the end of the first day of eight
hours' marching, they had covered approximately one and a quarter miles.

The following days passed in the same dreary and unrewarding routine. Never
entirely rested, their hunger never entirely satisfied, and their clothes always wet,
the men strained and slipped at their loads over the hummocked and slushy ice, averaging for hours of labor a mile and a half a day. Shackleton's plan had been that they
would pull west for sixty miles; by now, even he must have known they would never
make this mark.

"A harder or more discouraging march, I have never had the misfortune to participate in," wrote Bakewell.

On December 27, silent doubts and resentments became dramatically apparent.

"The skipper had trouble with the carpenter to-day whilst sledging," wrote Wordie. "To-night the company assembled on the floe, and the ship's articles were read." After struggling over a particularly bad section of ice for two hours, McNish dug in his heels and announced in abusive language he would go no farther.

Shackleton was up ahead with the pioneering party, and it was left to Worsley, who was in charge of the boat haulers, to tackle McNish. This he proved incapable of doing. There had always been tension between the two men; had the boat haulers been under the command of anyone else, the incident might not have arisen. In any case, a flustered Worsley sent for Shackleton, who hastened back from the head of the column.

McNish was exhausted, wet through, suffering from piles, and still heartsick over the loss of his pet, Mrs. Chippy. For weeks, he had complained that he had not been allowed to salvage wood from the *Endurance* to build a sloop that would carry them all to freedom. Others shared his disappointment. The old salt now turned sea lawyer, arguing that his duty to obey orders had terminated with the abandonment of the *Endurance*.

Hard words were exchanged between the two men. Technically, McNish's contention was correct. Nonetheless, Shackleton called a muster and read aloud the ship's articles, with a few elaborations of his own: He informed his men that they

Loaded Sledge

Sledges loaded with supplies—in this case, dog pemmican and cane sugar—were hauled by the dog teams on the march.

would be paid up until the day they reached safe port—not, as under normal articles, only until the loss of their ship. Consequently, the men were bound by his orders until that time.

McNish cooled down, and the situation passed. But Shackleton remained conscious of the narrowly averted danger. More had been at stake than one disgruntled seaman. Not only had McNish disobeyed orders at a moment of critically low morale, but he had also, as it were, defied Shackleton's optimistic pronouncements. It was now impossible to pretend that their painful efforts held any hope of success. Perhaps Shackleton's muttering critics had been right, and they should not have moved from Ocean Camp; perhaps Chippy should have built his sloop. McNish's brief rebellion had suggested the unthinkable—that the Boss was capable of significant error.

In this fraught context, Shackleton's reluctant decision to suspend the march two days later was both bitter and courageous. The ice ahead was completely unnegotiable, forcing not only a halt, but a retreat of half a mile to stronger footing. The men retired at 10 p.m., without a meal.

Patience Camp

Hurley and Shackleton sit before the entrance to their tent. Hurley (left) is skinning a penguin for fuel for the blubber stove between them, which he built.

"Turned in but could not sleep," Shackleton wrote in his diary. "Thought the whole matter over & decided to retreat to more secure ice: it is the only safe thing to do. . . . Am anxious. . . . Everyone working well except the carpenter: I shall never forget him in this time of strain & stress."

A sturdy-looking floe was chosen for the new camp; but the following day the opening of a deep crack forced them to shift again. The ice, they now discovered, was not as stable as it had been at their previous camp.

"All the floes in the neighborhood appear to be saturated by the sea to the very surface," wrote Worsley. "So much that on cutting 1 inch below the surface of a 6 or 7 feet thick floe, water almost at once flows into the hole." But the men were stuck; the floes behind them had disintegrated too much for further retreat.

A week's backbreaking labor had gained the party eight miles. Behind them, at Ocean Camp, lay additional stores, books, clothing, an efficient stove, wood for the floors of their tents—a comfortable routine. Moreover, the boats they dragged with them at such cost had been damaged by the journey.

"I heard the Carpenter say that if we had to go over much more such rough ice, the boats would not float when we did reach open water," Bakewell recalled. One can be sure McNish took pains to make this piece of information widely known. He had got his revenge; above all else, the sailors feared damage to the precious boats.

Despite all bitter setbacks and second thoughts, life on the floes had to be re-established. The tents were set up in a line along the treacherous snow, parallel to the dogs.

"We have called our camp Patience Camp," wrote Lees.

It was now January 1916, and still the pack showed no sign of breaking up. Moreover, the wind had stalled, keeping the crew just short of the 66th parallel. The days and weeks passed with renewed tedium and moody tension.

"Playing a game of wait almost wearies one's patience," Hurley wrote, with uncharacteristic impatience; he was normally as resilient to their circumstances as any member of the expedition. To pass the time, the men took walks around the perimeter of their floe, read, played bridge, and lay in their sleeping bags. McNish ostentatiously recaulked the damaged boats, using seal blood. Their predicament was now analyzed as it had not been before.

"The Boss at any rate has changed his mind yet once again," wrote Wordie dryly. "He now intends waiting for leads, and just as firmly believes he will get them, as he did a week ago that the ice would be fit for sledging the boats at the rate of ten miles a day." Shackleton himself was preoccupied and moody, and not at all amenable to well-intentioned suggestions. Lees was openly frantic over the state of their supplies, and daily roamed off on unauthorized seal hunts across the rotting ice; Worsley was eventually put in charge of "minding" him. Greenstreet's suggestion that every seal and penguin that approached the camp should be killed and stored was met with impatience by Shackleton.

"'Oh,' he said," according to Greenstreet, "'You're a bloody pessimist. That would put the wind up the fo'c'sle crowd, they'd think we were never going to get out.'" But food had become a real worry; seals had been

Sue's Pups—the Ikeys

At first the dogs had been merely sledging animals; but as the long months on the ice progressed they became companions, providing the men with their chief diversion. Hurley devotes an entire chapter to "Sledge Dog Pals" in his book Argonauts of the South.

scarce, and supplies of meat and blubber were dwindling.

On January 14, the teams of Wild, Crean, McIlroy, and Marston were shot, twenty-seven dogs in all. No more use was envisioned for them, and the food they consumed had become too valuable; their "dog pemmican" would become a staple of the men's diet.

"This duty fell upon me & was the worst job I ever had in my life," Wild reported. "I have known many men I would rather shoot than the worst of the dogs." This necessity upset all the men.

"One of the saddest events since we left Home," as McNish recorded. The same evening, Hurley and Macklin were authorized to make a dangerous run with their teams to Ocean Camp. With some difficulty, they returned with 900 pounds of stores the following day. This was the last run for Hurley's team.

"Wild shot my team during the afternoon," Hurley wrote, then bade farewell to his favorite dog. "Hail to thee old leader Shakespeare, I shall ever remember thee—fearless, faithful & diligent."

Hussey and Samson
The smallest member of the expedition and one of the biggest dogs.

At last, on January 21, after a month of maddening calm, a blizzard from the southwest blew them across the Antarctic Circle into familiar waters. They were now within 150 miles of Snow Hill Island, although very much to its east. Shackleton celebrated the occasion by issuing each man an extra bannock. Nevertheless, an excursion made some days later by Wordie and Worsley to a nearby berg revealed that the long-awaited breakup was nowhere in sight.

"Ice almost everywhere," Wordie reported, after having climbed the berg for a lookout position. Because seals were scarce, their stores of blubber were now dwindling. To conserve fuel, Shackleton cut down the daily ration of hot drinks to a single cup of tea in the morning.

At the end of January, the vagaries of the pack rotated their old Ocean Camp to within less than six miles—and ironically, in a more desirable westerly position than they themselves now held. On February 2, Shackleton authorized the retrieval of the third boat that had been left behind, the *Stancomb Wills*.

"It has taken a long time to persuade the Boss to this move," Wordie noted, "and I doubt if he would have done it, had it not been for the general feeling in camp." No one believed that the two boats alone could have contained the whole company. Shackleton had resisted authorizing the trip, being morbidly afraid of losing men to unnecessary accidents. But with all three boats safe in camp, everyone was in better spirits, the sailors in particular—although this was generally thought to be as much because of the big bundle of salvaged items they had secreted into their tent as to the arrival of the *Stancomb Wills*.

Time continued to drag on. Shackleton ordered the refuse pile of old seal bones, flippers, and discarded bits and pieces picked over for blubber. "The seal question" was getting very serious; they were now running short of not only blubber for fuel, but meat for food.

"So there is nothing for it but get into our sleeping bags. And smoke away the hunger," wrote McNish. "What [Prime Minister] Loyde George calls a luxery for working men."

Wet weather and driving snow kept the men inside their tents, while the tents themselves were more sodden than ever. The groundsheet of tent No. 5 had been commandeered to make a sail for one of the boats. In its stead, oilskin jackets and trousers, two blankets, and a sea leopard's skin were now all that lay between the sleeping bags and wet snow. Several of the tents had been rent by gales, and were in any case so thin that a gust of wind outside blew cigarette smoke within.

In early February, Lees was rebuked by Shackleton for making pessimistic statements.

"It is well to record these little sidelights on expeditionary life," wrote Lees, with no sign of ill feeling. "As they are usually expunged from the published books, or at most left to be read between the lines." Shackleton had continued to restrict Lees's seal-hunting excursions, claiming—incorrectly—that enough meat had been laid by to last a month. This restriction alienated even the loyal Worsley, and Shackleton's optimism was meeting with private cynicism on many fronts.

"His sublime optimism all the way thro being to my mind absolute foolishness," wrote Greenstreet. "Everything right away thro was going to turn out all right and no notice was taken of things possibly turning out otherwise and here we are." It is hard to judge Shackleton's rationale. He could not have been more keenly attuned to the moods of his men, and none of their discontent on this issue could have escaped him. Moreover, he was not one to let his pride prevent him from reversing a bad decision. Rather, Shackleton's dogged resistance to laying by more than a few weeks' supply of food was governed by a carefully reasoned ethic. His main concern was always for the morale of the sailors, and none of these men left diaries, so it is impossible to determine their state of mind. From other accounts one gleans suggestions that they were both more despondent and more troublesome than was ever directly stated. The wardroom members—the officers and scientists—had come south with the expectation of wintering on the ice, and of making sledging excursions. Lees's thoughts at the start of the ill-fated second march are illuminating.

"Were it not for a little natural anxiety as to our ultimate progress I have never been happier in my life than I am now, for is not this kind of existence the 'real thing,' the thing I have for years set my heart on. . . ." He had set his heart on a taste of the man-hauling epics of Scott's heroic age, and it was precisely for such an experience that many of the men had joined Shackleton. But not the sailors. Their lives centered on their ships, and their ship had been lost. And while they too had come south with Shackleton for adventure, sagas of man-hauling stoicism were not in their frames of reference. They did not wish to entertain the possibility of spending another winter on the ice; they wanted to take to the boats. Shackleton's prime objective was to keep his men unified—and this may have necessitated some apparently illogical decisions.

Towards the end of February, the sudden appearance of a flock of little Adélie penguins came as a boon to the hungry men. Three hundred were taken. Their flesh served as food, their skins as fuel for the galley stove. The temperatures had started to fall, and the men complained of feeling cold even in their bags.

"I have had no sleep for the last to nights with the cold," wrote McNish. Shackleton visited the tents in turn, settling in each to spin yarns, recite poetry, or play bridge.

"The food now is pretty well all meat," Greenstreet wrote. "Seal steaks, stewed seal, penguin steaks, stewed penguin, penguin liver. . . . The cocoa has been finished for some time and the tea is very nearly done. . . . Flour also is very nearly finished." With Lees and Green, the cook, Shackleton fretted over the daily menu, conspiring with them ways to make it more satisfying. Seals and penguins permitting, "special occasions" were celebrated to break the monotony.

"In honour of Leap Year Day & the escape of some of our batchelors from the Fair Sex, we have 3 full meals with a hot beverage to each," Worsley wrote on February 29, "and so we all feel well fed & happy tonight."

The drift of the pack was once again averaging two miles per day. By early March they were only seventy miles from Paulet Island. Snow Hill Island already lay behind them.

On March 7, a blizzard arose, the heaviest snowfall since they had entered the ice. Too cold to read or play cards, the men lay in the tents, huddled in bags that had frozen as stiff as sheet iron. Two days later, digging out sledges and gear from the four feet of drift that had fallen, a curious motion was detected in the pack: the swell of the ocean beneath them. The following day, Shackleton organized drills to practice loading the boats, so as to be ready at a moment's notice in the event their floe broke under them.

The ice parted some days later, but then quickly closed again. Still they drifted north, moving farther and farther up the Palmer Peninsula. They were drawing abreast of Paulet Island.

March 21 marked the first day of winter. The hours of light shrank each day as the weather grew colder. On the morning of March 23, Shackleton sighted land to the west. "There has been a lot of doubt in the skipper's part," wrote McNish, with sardonic satisfaction. "As he never saw it first. After being on the look out this last 2 months & reporting so many bergs as being land he is feeling quite sick over it being seen by any one else." But it was true land—the jagged, snow-covered ridges of Joinville Island, the first land the men had seen in sixteen months.

"If the ice opens we could land in a day," Hurley wrote. But the ice didn't open. Still the pack held, too loose to cross on foot, too close to sail, and still it drifted north. Day by day, Shackleton silently watched as his worst fears were realized. They were approaching the very farthest tip of the Palmer Peninsula; soon there would be no more land ahead.

On March 30, the last of the dogs were shot, and the younger ones eaten. There were no expressions of regret this time, only grim acceptance of the necessity and pleasure at the unexpected tastiness of their meat. Several big seals were also killed, and the men had their first good feed in two weeks. The sledging rations were still held, relatively untouched, in reserve.

"Such a life ages one," Hurley noted in his diary. That same night, March 31, their floe was riven by a crack that separated the men from the boats. Shackleton set all hands on "watch and watch"—half the camp on duty at all times—but the ice held throughout the rest of the night. Days of heavy wind followed, and the men lay in their bags with nothing to do but talk, while the floe bumped under them. Lees became seasick.

Worsley's sightings indicated that the floe was travelling faster than the wind was blowing it; evidently the disintegrating pack was now in the grip of strong currents. At dawn on April 7, daylight revealed the precipitous snow-streaked mountains of Clarence Island; later in the day, the sharp peaks of Elephant Island showed just west of north. With almost bewildering speed, the drift now carried them directly north towards the islands. It then veered alarmingly to the west, beyond striking range of either island; then swerved east again, bringing the two islands directly ahead. Every day saw new contingencies and necessitated new plans. Wildlife became abundant, with gulls, petrels, and terns overhead, and whales blowing in the leads.

On the evening of April 8, the ice cracked once again, right under the *James Caird*. Pitching like a ship at sea, the floe broke down to a triangle measuring some 90 by 100 by 120 yards.

"I felt that the time for launching the boats was near at hand," wrote Shackleton. After breakfast on April 9, camp was struck, and the boats prepared. The men ate a last good meal while standing at the ready.

At 1 p.m., Shackleton gave the long-awaited order to launch the boats. Positions had been designated months before: The *James Caird*, the large whaler, was commanded by Shackleton and Wild, and on board were Clark, Hurley, Hussey, James, Wordie, McNish, Green, Vincent, and McCarthy. In the *Dudley Docker*, under the command of Worsley, were Greenstreet, Kerr, Lees, Macklin, Cheetham, Marston, McLeod, and Holness. And in the smallest and least seaworthy boat, the *Stancomb Wills*, Rickinson, McIlroy, How, Bakewell, Blackborow, and Stephenson were under the command of Hudson and Crean.

At 1:30 p.m., the boats pushed off. There was a heavy swell, and the lanes of open water zigzagged erratically between the lurching floes.

"Our first day in the water was one of the coldest and most dangerous of the expedition," wrote Bakewell. "The ice was running riot. It was a hard race to keep our boats in the open leads. . . . [W]e had many narrow escapes from being crushed when the larger masses of the pack would come together."

The men had been trapped in the ice for fifteen months. But their real ordeal had just begun.

First landing on Elephant Island

April, 15, 1915: Solid land after 497 days on ice and sea. "The Boss, the Skipper, the cook and Hurley went on board the 'Wills,' and helped her crew to take her up a small creek in the rocks. . . . She then made trips to and fro under Tom Crean's charge." (Wordie, diary)

Into the Boats

4–10–16

Last night, a night of tension & anxiety—on a par with the night of the ship's destruction. . . . Sea & wind increase & have to draw up onto an old isolated floe and pray to God it will remain entire throughout the night. No sleep for 48 Hours, all wet Cold & miserable with a N.E. Blizzard raging . . . no sight of land & Pray for cessation of these wild conditions.

—FRANK HURLEY, *diary*

In the gathering dusk of the first night at sea, Shackleton and his men camped on a floe measuring some 200 by 100 feet, which rocked visibly in the ocean swell. Darkness came early, at around 7 p.m., but it was a mild evening, with the temperature around 18°. After a hot meal cooked by Green on the blubber stove, the men retired to their tents.

"Some intangible feeling of uneasiness made me leave my tent about 11 p.m. that night and glance around the quiet camp," Shackleton wrote. "I started to walk across the floes in order to warn the watchman to look carefully for cracks, and as I was passing the men's tent the floe lifted on the crest of a swell and cracked right under my feet." As Shackleton watched, the crack ran beneath the sailors' tent and emptied How and Holness, who was still in his bag, into the water. How struggled out, and Shackleton, grasping Holness's bag, hove it onto the ice before the edges of the floe clamped together again.

There was no more sleep that night. Hudson generously offered dry clothes to Holness, who was grumbling that he had lost his tobacco. Shackleton issued hot milk and Streimer's Polar Nut Food—a treat from the uncracked sledging rations—to all hands, who huddled around the blubber stove. From the leads of dark water around them, the blowing of the killer whales punctuated the long hours of the night.

When dawn broke at 6 a.m., the men discovered that the floe was surrounded by loose ice. While all hands waited anxiously for an opening to clear, a dangerous swell was growing, crashing the ice fragments together, as Lees noted, "with a force sufficient to smash a moderately sized yacht."

By the time the boats were launched at 8 a.m., the wind was high and squally, at times reaching gale force. For two hours the men rowed against the heavy swell through a tortuous network of channels and leads, then through "survival ice," old hummocky floes and brash at the outer margins of the pack. The crew's all-meat diet had taken a toll, as Lees had predicted. Lacking even minimal carbohydrates over the past months, the men working the oars were soon exhausted.

A light haze had descended upon an otherwise mild day, obscuring their intended landfall, Clarence or Elephant island, now a mere sixty or so miles distant. The overloaded, unwieldy boats did not allow for refinements in navigation. The *Stancomb Wills* in particular was already cause for grave concern, lacking "the canvas" to keep abreast of her more seaworthy companions. Shackleton had given orders that all three were to stay in hailing distance of one another, but this was not always easily accomplished.

Amid towering icebergs of fantastic shapes, the boats nosed their way closer and closer towards the edge of the ice. But when they finally broke triumphantly through it, they were hit head-on by a high sea unbuffered by the pack; abruptly, Shackleton ordered them back inside. Reluctant to head due north through open, running sea, they now turned their course west, towards King George Island.

At dusk, the boats turned to a circular floe, some twenty yards across, and made camp. Later in the night, the wind rose, dropping snow and rocking their camp with heavy swell. Chunks of the floe broke off in the wind-whipped waves, but Shackleton, who had remained up all night with the watchman, McNish, deemed the camp to be in no immediate danger, and let the men sleep—or try to. Hurley's diary indicates there were no illusions inside the tents about the safety of their position.

By dawn, a huge swell was running under overcast, misty skies that turned to snowy squalls. Heaving undulations of ice swept towards them. Shackleton, Worsley, and Wild took turns climbing to the peak of their rocking berg, searching for a break of open water in the ice, while the men stood by the boats and waited. As the hours passed, their floe, grinding against loose pack, became gradually smaller.

"One of the anxieties in my mind was the possibility that we would be driven by the current through the eighty-mile gap between Clarence Island and Prince George Island [as it was then called] into the open Atlantic," wrote Shackleton. By noon, the squalls had slackened, and when a lane of open water appeared, the boats rushed into it. They had set out late in the day; with dusk falling at 5 p.m., few hours of light remained for sailing, and come nightfall they were still amid the loose pack. As before, a suitable floe was found for a camp, and Green and his blubber stove were disembarked. But it quickly became apparent that the floe could not serve them through the night, and Shackleton reluctantly determined that they would have to sleep in the boats.

Several hours of desultory rowing brought them under the lee of a heavy old floe, where the boats were moored alongside one another for the night.

"Constant rain and snow squalls blotted out the stars and soaked us through," Shackleton wrote. "Occasionally the ghostly shadows of silver, snow, and fulmar petrels flashed close to us, and all around we could hear the killers blowing, their short, sharp hisses sounding like sudden escapes of steam." A school of killer whales had languidly drifted around the boats, their sleek, sinister black forms surrounding them on every side for the duration of the long night. Of all the memories the men would carry with them, this—the slow, measured rising of the white-throated whales in the dark waters around their boats—remained one of the most terrible and abiding. In their long months on the ice, the men had borne abundant witness to the great beasts' ice-shattering power. Whether they would attack humans, no one really knew. For the men, these were prodigies of the deep, mysterious and evil, possessed of chilling reptilian eyes that betrayed disconcerting mammalian intelligence. Seasick and sleepless, the men bumped and jostled endlessly amid the ice and whales. It was this night that began to break the will of many.

Regarding his companions in the cold dawn that followed, Shackleton noted simply that "the strain was beginning to tell." He promised a hot breakfast, and the men manned the oars to seek out a suitable floe, their frozen Burberry suits crackling and shedding shards of ice as they pulled. At eight o'clock, the "galley" was landed on a floe; by nine o'clock they were under way again. Around them, basking in the welcome sunshine, hundreds of seals lounged comfortably on floes flushed pink by the sunrise.

They had been travelling roughly northwest since the day they left Patience Camp. Now, under hazy sunshine, Worsley balanced himself against the mast of the *Dudley Docker* to take the first noon observation the weather had allowed. Expectations were high as to the miles gained. But the results were worse than anyone would have dreamed possible.

"A terrible disappt.," wrote Worsley in his diary. Not a single mile had been gained. Instead, they had drifted back to the southeast—thirty miles *east* of their position at Patience Camp and eleven miles south. A strong easterly current concealed by the heavy swell, combined with a tortuous navigation through sinuous lanes, had obscured all sense of direction.

Shackleton tried to downplay the bad news, saying only that they had not "done as well as expected." It was three in the afternoon, and dusk came at five. King George and Deception islands, to the west, were now out of reach. Elephant Island, to the north, the closest land, lay outside the pack, in high seas; behind them to the southwest, Hope Bay, on the tip of the Palmer Peninsula, was 130 miles away in water that was for the moment clear. After consulting with Worsley and Wild, Shackleton opted to take advantage of the northwest wind and turn the boats back towards Hope Bay.

By nightfall, they found themselves amid loose, fragmented ice in a choppy sea. The weather was becoming colder and wetter, and as on the previous night, no floe could be found large enough to establish a camp. Eventually, the boats were tethered one behind the other and moored to the lee side of a large chunk of ice.

At nine o'clock, a shift in the wind blew back the clouds, revealing a bright moon but also driving the boats against the jagged floe. Hastily, the painter of the lead boat, the *James Caird*, was cut, and with no other mooring available, the three small vessels drifted through the night in a sea of brash ice. The temperature had dropped, and new pancakes of ice had formed on the water's surface.

Shivering together in each other's arms, some of the men tried to snatch minutes of sleep; many preferred to row or fend off the chunks of ice that sped their way— anything to keep their cold arms moving.

"Occasionally from an almost clear sky came snow-showers," wrote Shackleton, "falling silently on the sea and laying a thin shroud of white over our bodies and our boats." Lees, in the *Dudley Docker*, had appropriated the only complete set of oilskins, which he adamantly refused to share. As his snoring indicated, he for one found sleep possible.

When a foggy dawn at last put an end to the night, the crew discovered that the boats were sheathed in ice, inside and out. The temperature in the night had dropped to −7°. As the ice was hacked off with axes, lumps were distributed for the men to eat.

"Most of the men were now looking seriously worn and strained," Shackleton wrote. "Their lips were cracked and their eyes and eyelids showed red in their salt-encrusted faces. . . . Obviously, we must make land quickly, and I decided to run for Elephant Island."

The wind had shifted again, blowing now from the southeast. Shackleton's decision to change course again and, at any cost, make for the nearest land was determined by the realization that he was now racing for the very lives of many of his men. He could no longer afford the luxury of caution. As the boats ran before the wind for Elephant Island, a man in the bow of each attempted to fend away lumps of brash while they plunged precariously down leads in the thin new ice. The wind grew stronger, and the boats made their way once again to the edge of the pack, and by noon had crashed into deep sapphire waters. With the sun out, the wind favorable and strong, they raced towards their destination.

By four in the afternoon, the wind had increased to a gale that blew surging waves into the boats, compounding the men's misery. The *Stancomb Wills* alone had not had her gunwales raised, and water poured in over stores and men. From the *James Caird*, Shackleton, sensing a need to lift morale if only in some small way, distributed extra food to all hands. A number, overcome with seasickness, could not take advantage of this bonus; many were suffering from dysentery from uncooked dog pemmican, and were forced to relieve themselves over the side of the surging boats, balancing on the gunwales.

Shackleton's order that the boats stay in hailing distance of one another became increasingly difficult to obey. The *Stancomb Wills* was knee-deep in water, and Holness, one of the trawlerhands who previously made his living braving the icy north Atlantic, covered his face and wept with sheer terror and misery. Worsley, drawing abreast of the *James Caird*, suggested to Shackleton that they run through the night; but Shackleton, wary as ever of splitting his party, and afraid they might even overrun the island in the darkness, gave the order to lay to. It was a hard decision to make.

"I doubted if all the men would survive that night," he stated simply. On top of all else, they had no water. Usually, ice was taken on board at each "campsite," but the hasty departure from the veering floe the night before had made this impossible. Tormented by the salt spray flung continually in their faces, the men's mouths were swollen and their lips bloody. Frozen raw seal meat provided the only relief.

Sea anchors, made of canvas and oars lashed together, were flung overboard, and there began the third night in the boats. Through all the demanding days and all the long and terrible hours of darkness, the helmsmen—Wild and McNish, Hudson and Crean, Worsley and Greenstreet—had remained immovable at their posts as waves crashed over them, as their clothes froze upon them, as the wind and spray stung their tired faces.

The wind subsided in the night, and at dawn the sleepless men beheld the glorious mauve sunrise that flashed on the eastern horizon; and only thirty miles directly ahead lay Clarence Island, its snow-clad peak glowing in the dawn. Later, in full daylight, Elephant Island appeared, exactly on the bearings that Worsley had calculated, in Shackleton's words, "with two days' dead reckoning while following a devious course through the pack-ice and after drifting during two nights at the mercy of wind and waves." Elephant Island was the less precipitous of the two; additionally, it lay to windward, ensuring that if the boats missed their first attempted landfall, they would have Clarence Island as alternative to their lee.

The night had taken its toll.

"At least half of the party were insane," according to Wild, "fortunately not violent, simply helpless and hopeless." The *Stancomb Wills* drew abreast of the *Caird* to report that Hudson had collapsed after seventy-two hours at the helm, and Blackborow reported that "there was something wrong" with his feet. Continual immersion in salt water had caused the eruption of painful boils on many men; their bodies were badly chafed, and their mouths throbbed with thirst. As the wind died they took to the oars, a task made painful by the blisters on their hands. By three in the afternoon, the boats were only ten miles from land, the harsh glaciers and icy mountains of Elephant Island now discernable in fine detail. At this point, the men encountered a strong tidal current that held the boats at bay. After a solid hour of rowing at the pitch of their strength, they were not so much as a mile closer to the island.

At five o'clock, lowering skies to the northwest darkened, and shortly afterward a storm broke. There would be no landfall after all, but another night in the pitching boats.

"We were in the midst of confused lumpy seas which running . . . from two directions were far more dangerous for small boats than the straight running waves of a heavy gale in open seas," Worsley wrote. "The boats could never settle down, and to steer became a work of art."

Now all three boats were bailed continuously; in the belabored *Stancomb Wills*, four of the eight men were completely incapacitated: McIlroy, How, and Bakewell bailed through the night for their lives and those of their shipmates, while Crean held the tiller. In the *James Caird*, McNish relieved Wild at the helm, but briefly fell asleep, exhausted. Wild, unshaken, unchanged, took over again, "his steel-blue eyes," as Shackleton recorded with affectionate pride, looking "out to the day ahead." In the *Docker*, around midnight, Cheetham heard the boat's back cracking, and all hands scurried to shift their stores. Huddled under the canvas of one of the tents, Greenstreet managed to light a match so that Worsley could glimpse his tiny compass. Later, some of the crew noticed that Worsley himself did not seem to hear them anymore, that his head was sinking on his chest. When at last he was persuaded to surrender the helm to Greenstreet, he was so stiff from hunching over the tiller that he could not unbend, and his rigid muscles had to be massaged before he could lie straight on the bottom of the boat: He had not slept for more than ninety hours.

"It was," wrote Shackleton, "a stern night." The *James Caird* had taken the limping *Stancomb Wills* in tow, though at times the latter was lost to sight, vanishing into the deep trough of the swell, then reemerging from the black sea, tossed on the crest of a wave. The survival of the *Wills*, the least sound of the boats, depended upon her keeping contact with the *Caird*, and throughout the night Shackleton sat with his hand on her painter, as it grew heavy with ice. He must have been very near exhaustion.

"Practically ever since we had first started Sir Ernest had been standing erect day and night on the stern-counter of the *Caird*," Lees wrote. "How he stood the incessant vigil and exposure is marvelous." Shackleton had not slept since leaving Patience Camp.

A sudden heavy squall of snow hid the boats from one another, and when it cleared, the *Dudley Docker* was gone; she had vanished into the darkness and the racing sea. For Shackleton, this was perhaps the worst moment of the journey.

When the dawn came at last, the air was so thick with mist that the men aboard the *Caird* and the *Wills* were under the cliffs of Elephant Island before they saw them. Anxiously, they followed the precipitous coastline until at 9 a.m. they sighted a narrow beach at the northwest end of the island, beyond a fringe of surf-beaten rocks.

"I decided we must face the hazards of this unattractive landing-place," wrote Shackleton. "Two days and nights without drink or hot food had played havoc with most of the men." His own throat and tongue were so swollen he could only whisper, and his orders were passed along by either Wild or Hurley. Shackleton boarded the *Wills* to take her through first, and as he did so the *Dudley Docker* hove in sight.

"This," wrote Shackleton, "took a great load off my mind."

The *Wills* was carefully positioned at an opening in the reef, then shot through on the top of waves to the rough stony beach beyond. Shackleton gave the word that Blackborow, as the youngest member of the expedition, should have the honor of being the first to land; but Blackborow sat motionless.

"In order to avoid delay I helped him, perhaps a little roughly, over the side of the boat," wrote Shackleton. "He promptly sat down in the surf and did not move. Then I suddenly realized what I had forgotten, that both his feet were frost-bitten badly."

The *Docker* followed the *Wills*, and then the *James Caird*, too heavy to land, was unloaded in tedious relays before being taken through the reef and beached beside the other boats.

The men staggered onto land. With his Vest Pocket Kodak camera in hand, Hurley bounded out to record the landing of the boats and the first meal on Elephant Island.

"Some of the men were reeling about the beach as if they had found an unlimited supply of alcoholic liquor on the desolate island," Shackleton wrote. His bemused, paternal tone conjures an almost comical scene of readjustment; but the diaries hint darkly at the journey's actual toll.

"Many suffered from temporary aberration," Hurley reported, "walking aimlessly about; others shivering as with palsy." "Hudson," McNish states with characteristic directness, "has gone of[f] his head."

Some filled their pockets with stones, or rolled along the shingled beach, burying their faces in the stones and pouring handfuls over them.

"In the *Wills*, only two men were fit to do anything," Wordie recorded. "Some fellows moreover were half crazy: one got an axe and did not stop till he had killed about ten seals. . . . None of us suffered like this in the *Caird*."

On Elephant Island

The James Caird, Dudley Docker, *and* Stancomb Wills *safely ashore at Cape Valentine,*
Elephant Island. The men pull the Caird *to higher ground; two figures, one in the distance, can be seen*
seated to the left of the boat, one of whom is probably Blackborow, crippled by frostbite. Off-loaded
supplies can be seen on the beach above the boats.

They had spent seven fearful days in open boats in the South Atlantic, at the beginning of an Antarctic winter; 170 days drifting on a floe of ice with inadequate food and shelter; and not since December 5, 1914—497 days before—had they set foot on land.

After meals of seal steaks, the men laid their bags on the solid earth and turned in for the night.

"I did not sleep much," Bakewell recalled, "just lay in my damp sleeping bag and relaxed. It was hard for me to realize that I was on good old solid earth once more. I got up several times during the night and joined the others, who were like me, just too happy to sleep. We would gather around the fire, eat and drink a little, have a smoke and talk over some of the past adventures."

As they would soon discover, they had arrived on an abnormally fine day. Elephant Island offered salvation, but a grimmer or more hostile piece of land was difficult to conceive. The narrow shingle beach onto which they had drawn the boats offered little protection from high seas, and the morning after landing, Wild set out with Marston, Crean, Vincent, and McCarthy in the *Dudley Docker* to scout the coast for a better camp. He returned in the evening, after dark, with the news that there was a suitable place seven miles down the north coast. At daybreak on the 17th, the weary men loaded up the boats, leaving many boxes of sledging rations stacked against the rocks. No one had the energy to load them—and this at least ensured an emergency supply of provisions in the event a second boat journey was required. Shortly after they shoved off, another gale arose, threatening to sweep the boats out to sea.

Elephant Island

Cape Valentine is thought to have got its name because the sealer-explorer who charted the South Shetlands in the early nineteenth century came through on St. Valentine's Day.

"Scenically, our present environments are some of the grandest I have ever set eyes on. Cliffs that throw their serrated scarps a thousand feet into the skies are interspersed with glaciers that tumble in crevassed cascades down to the sea. Here they present walls of blue ice 100 to 180 feet in height."

(Hurley, diary)

"Weathered what we call the Castle Rock and finally reached our destination," wrote Wordie, "more exhausted I think, than by the previous boat journey."

The new camp offered a somewhat larger, gravelly beach, but was still foreboding.

"Such a wild & inhospitable coast I have never beheld," Hurley wrote upon their arrival, and evoked the "vast headland, black and menacing that rose from a seething surf 1,200 feet above our heads & so sheer as to have the appearance of overhanging." On the other hand, wildlife was abundant, with seals, gentoo and ringed penguins, and even limpets in the shallow waters, although no sign of the elephant seal from which the island took its name.

Many of the men were still incapacitated. The most critical were Blackborow with severe frostbite, Hudson with frostbite and a mysterious pain in his lower back, and Rickinson, who was believed to have suffered a heart attack. The others on the sick list were simply "stove in."

After meals of seal steaks and hot milk, the men pitched their flimsy tents as high above the tidal mark of their new camp as possible, and retired to their wet sleeping bags. But a blizzard rose in the night, ripping the largest tent to ribbons and bringing the others down flat. Some of the men crawled into the boats; others simply lay under the collapsed tents, with the cold, wet canvas draped across their faces. The wind was severe enough to blow around the beached *Dudley Docker*—"and she is a heavy boat," as Lees noted. Precious gear was lost to this unexpected gale, including aluminum cooking pans and a bag of spare warm underclothing—blown away to parts unknown.

On the 19th, with the blizzard still in full spate, the men were awakened by Shackleton bringing them their breakfast.

"The Boss is wonderful," wrote Wordie, "cheering everyone and far more active than any other person in camp." At least there was now plenty of food, and the men consumed prodigious amounts of blubber and seal steak. Hurley, Clark, and Greenstreet were enlisted as cooks, Green being one of the men on "the sick list."

With shelter nonexistent, the sleeping bags were now sodden. The heat of the men's bodies melted not just the snow underneath them, but the frozen, reeking guano of the penguin rookery on which they lay.

For months the men had dreamt of land, and for long days and nights in the boats they had fought for it. But now the hard truth dawned on them that the conditions they had so far encountered on this particular piece of land did not represent some terrible aberration, or a run of atrocious weather; this was the way it was going to be as long as they were on Elephant Island. On April 19, a quiet rebellion against these cruel circumstances occurred among the sailors.

"Some of the men were showing signs of demoralization," Shackleton noted. They had neglected to place their gloves and hats inside their shirts during the night, with the result that these items were frozen solid come morning—demonstrating, as Shackleton stated, "the proverbial carelessness of the sailor." They used this negligence as an excuse not to do any work.

"Only by rather drastic methods were they induced to turn to," wrote Shackleton. What happened here? As at Patience Camp, the diaries leave one with a sense that all the facts have not been plainly spoken.

"Some of the party . . . had become despondant," wrote Wild, "& were in a 'What's the use' sort of mood & had to be driven to work, none too gently either." Wordie says, almost in passing, that "dejected men were dragged from their bags and set to work." Hurley's pointed diary entry on this day, however, is blistering:

On April 17, Shackleton led the men back out to sea and around to a spit of land seven miles to the west of their landing, which Frank Wild had discovered. The second campsite became known as Cape Wild—Cape Bloody Wild by the sailors—after both its "founder" and its weather. A blizzard raged for five straight days after the crew's landing.

Elephant Island

*"Such a wild & inhospitable
coast I have never beheld. Yet
there is a profound grandeur
about these savage cliffs with the
drifting snow & veiling
clouds. . . . I thought of those
lines of Service.—*

'A land of savage
grandeur
that measures each man
at his Worth.'"

(Hurley, diary)

Now that the party are established at an immovable base I review their general behaviour during the memorable escape from the ice. . . . It is regrettable to state that many conducted themselves in a manner unworthy of gentlemen & British sailors. . . . Of a fair proportion of the [company] I am convinced they would starve or freeze if left to their own resources on this island, for there is such an improvident disregard for their equipment, as to allow it to be buried in snow, or be carried off by the winds. Those who shirk duties, or lack a fair sense of practicability should not be in these parts. These are harsh places where it takes all one's time & energies to attend to the individual, & so make himself as effective & useful a unit as possible.

It was perhaps no coincidence that Shackleton chose the following day, April 20, to gather his company to make a momentous announcement: A party of men under his command would shortly set out in the *James Caird* and make for the whaling stations of South Georgia. The stupendous difficulties of this journey required no elaboration to the men who had just arrived on Elephant Island. The island of South Georgia was 800 miles away—more than ten times the distance they had just travelled. To reach it, a twenty-two-and-a-half-foot long open boat would have to cross the most formidable ocean on the planet, in the winter. They could expect winds up to 80 miles an hour, and heaving waves—the notorious Cape Horn Rollers—measuring from trough to crest as much as sixty feet in height; if unlucky, they would encounter worse. They would be navigating towards a small island, with no points of land in between, using a sextant and chronometer—under brooding skies that might not permit a single navigational sighting. The task was not merely formidable; it was, as every sailing man of the company knew, impossible.

"There is a party of 6 going to Georgia in the *Caird*," wrote McNish. "The party includes

> Sir Ernest
> Skipper
> Creen
> Macnish
> McCarthy
> Vincent."

The pride with which this concise entry is made is palpable. After he announced his plans, Shackleton had called McNish over to examine the *Caird* and asked him whether she could be made more seaworthy.

"He first enquired if he was to go with me," Shackleton reported, "and seemed quite pleased when I said 'Yes.'" There is no evidence that any of the men chosen faced the prospect of the new ordeal with anything but matter-of-fact determination and satisfaction. Crean, indeed, had begged to be included, although Wild had wanted him to remain with him. Shackleton, it is true—as Lees took pains to inform him—could possibly have waited out the winter and then attempted to cross back the way they had just come to the whaling waters near Deception Island; but this option meant many long, fickle months of delay. Besides, the first boat journey had

On April 20, Shackleton announced that he would attempt to sail the twenty-two-and-a-half-foot-long James Caird *to South Georgia, 800 miles away. Immediately, McNish set to work adapting the boat for its momentous journey. On April 21, McNish wrote in his diary, "All hands are busy skining & storing penguins. Some repairing the Cairds gear 2 sewing canvas for the deck. Myself Marsten & McLeod are busy getting the Caird ready. . . . There are 5 on the sick list some heart trouble some frost bites & 1 dilly." The negative for this photograph has been retouched, but apparently only to highlight faded details, rather than to change them.*

set him in motion, put him on a course from which there was now, it seemed, no turning back.

"Shackleton sitting still and doing nothing wasn't Shackleton at all," wrote Macklin. "We'd had all that at Patience Camp." Moreover, with his eye ever on the sailors, the Boss may have calculated that another long, demoralizing waiting game was not feasible; psychologically, it was better to offer his men the hope of even the longest of long shots.

The crew of the *James Caird* was chosen with care. Worsley had proved himself a gifted navigator. McNish would be useful as both shipwright and sailor—his rebellion on the ice notwithstanding, he was, with Crean, Vincent, and McCarthy (also Marston and Hurley), one of the handful of men whose performance during the boat journey had been singled out by Shackleton for commendation. Furthermore, Shackleton was once again gathering the potential troublemakers—Vincent and McNish—into his own safekeeping. Finally, in Crean, Shackleton knew he had a man who would persevere until the very bitter end.

Although the weather was still severe, all able hands now turned to equipping the lifeboat for its sea voyage. For the next few days, as the wind raged and driving snow fell, McNish was at work, mending a hole made by the ice in the boat's bow above the waterline and constructing a makeshift "decking." The timber available, salvaged from the freeboard of the *Dudley Docker* and other odds and ends, fell short of what was required, and so in lieu of an entire deck he assembled a frame to be covered with a spare bolt of canvas.

"Cheetham and McCarthy have been busy trying to stretch the canvas for the deck & They had rather a job as it was frozen stiff," wrote McNish. The canvas was thawed, foot by foot, over the blubber stove, allowing the brittle needles to be pushed and pulled through the heavy fabric with a pair of pincers. Heavy, wet snow fell throughout the day as they worked, and Wild, of all people, was overheard to say that if the weather continued much longer "some of the party will undoubtedly go under."

On the 22nd, McNish, working with few tools and frost-nipped hands, completed his task. The blizzard finally ceased, although heavy snow continued to fall as all able hands gathered round to look over his masterful handiwork.

"The carpenter had contrived wonderfully with the very limited resources at hand," wrote Lees. "She has been strengthened in the hull by having the mast of the *Dudley Docker* lashed along her keel inside." The *Caird* carried two masts: a mainmast, rigged with a standing lugsail and jib, and a mizzenmast, also lug rigged.

The foul weather held over the next two days, but moderated on the 24th, and Shackleton decided to launch the *Caird*. Having no ballast keel, the boat was ballasted with 1,500 pounds of shingle-filled bags made of blankets, and an additional 500 pounds of boulders. Worsley believed the ballast excessive and was concerned the boat would ride low and ship water—her freeboard was two feet two inches; Shackleton's fear was that a light boat would be in danger of capsizing in the high seas he knew they would face. The *Caird* also carried four oars and a pump that Hurley had made back at Ocean Camp from the binnacle of the *Endurance*. Additionally, bags of blubber oil were taken to pour on rough water, to prevent the breaking of waves.

Two barrels of melted ice were stowed along with the provisions. According to Hurley, these included:

The bosun of the <u>Endurance</u> mends a net, 1915

A former trawlerman who had worked in the North Atlantic, John Vincent was physically the strongest man on the Endurance. *His bullying manner had already caused friction, but he had held up better than most in the first boat journey to Elephant Island. Shackleton wanted him on board the* Caird *for his strength, seamanship—and to ensure that he would not cause trouble on Elephant Island.*

The Endurance

30 Boxes Matches

8 Galls. Petroleum

1 tin Spirit

10 boxes flamers

1 box blue lights

2 Primus Stoves & parts & Prickers

1 Cooker Complete

6 sleeping bags

Spare apparel (clothes sox, etc.)

Food

3 Cases Sledging ration = 300 rations

2 Nut foods = 200 rations

2 Biscuits—300 in case

1 case lump sugar

30 packets trumilk

1 tin Bovril Cubes

1 tin Cerebos Salt

36 galls Water

112 lbs. ice

Insts. Sextant, Binoculars, Compass, Candles, Blubber Oil for Oil Bag, sea anchor, charts. Fishing line & triangle, twine & needle. Bit of blubber for bait. Boathook, Aneroid.

Launching the <u>Caird</u>

The decking of the Caird *was completed on the morning of April 24, and as the weather was good, Shackleton decided to get under way as soon as possible. Here the men gather around the boat, preparatory to launching her. The* Stancomb Wills, *which was used to ferry supplies to the* Caird *for loading, is beached to the right.*

Launching the <u>Caird</u>

"Monday April 24 A fine morning I started on the boat at day break & finished at 10 A.M. Then all hands were mustered & we launched her."
(McNish, diary)

Shackleton also took his double-barrelled shotgun and some cartridges, and two axes. McNish took some of his remaining tools, including a carpenter's adze.

The food supplies were calculated to last four weeks.

"For if we did not make South Georgia in that time," wrote Shackleton, "we were sure to go under." The charts were those Worsley had ripped from books in the library of the *Endurance*, before she was abandoned.

Should the relief expedition fail, Wild was under orders to make his way in the remaining boats to Deception Island in the spring. Meanwhile, he was in sole com-

Launching the <u>Caird</u>

"As we were getting her of the beach a heavy surf came up & owing to us being unable to get her up of the beach she almost capsised as it was she emptyed Myself & Vincent overboard."
(McNish, diary)

"Great difficulty was experienced in keeping her off the labyrinth of rocks & reefs which abound along the treacherous foreshores" (Hurley, diary). The Caird carried two masts, and although there are no photographs or descriptions of her sails, it is thought that she was lug-rigged—that is, her sails were four-cornered and held from the mast by an oblique yard arm.

mand of the men left behind. He too had begged to make the journey, but there was no other person—on Elephant Island or anywhere else—whom Shackleton so implicitly trusted as Frank Wild. He knew this man would undertake nothing that Shackleton himself would not. The two men talked late into the night, Shackleton laying on last-minute injunctions, and Wild, imperturbable, giving his silent assent.

The *Caird* was taken out beyond the reef, where supplies were ferried to her by the *Stancomb Wills*, to the accompaniment of a running stream of banter and rough joking.

"Many were solicitous that . . . my behaviour on reaching civilization should be above reproach," wrote Worsley. "As for Crean; they said things that ought to have made him blush—but what would make Crean blush would make a butchers dog drop its bone." Taking advantage of the rare sunshine and clear horizon, Worsley had spent his last morning on land rating his chronometer.

A bad swell was running, and Marston, Greenstreet, Kerr, and Wild, who were carrying supplies through the surf, became wet to their waists. An early accident nearly put an end to the whole venture: While her crew were standing on her to load provisions, the *Caird* rolled heavily, nearly capsizing, and pitched McNish and Vincent into the water. Volunteers offered to exchange dry clothes with the men, but McNish refused, as only his trousers were wet; Vincent was wet through, and although he exchanged his trousers with How, he refused to take off his jersey.

"His refusal to change . . . called forth some unfavorable comments as to the reason," wrote Lees, "and it was freely stated that he had a good deal of other people's property concealed about his person." How's wet trousers would take two weeks to

dry. Shackleton deeply regretted the mishap, knowing it would be taken as an ill omen by the men left behind.

A band of ice along the north coast had steadily extended east for several days. Fearful that it would soon surround the island and prevent all escape, Shackleton was anxious to be under way. After smoking a last cigarette with Wild and shaking hands with his men, he boarded the *Stancomb Wills* and was ferried out to the waiting *Caird;* at 12:30 p.m., without ceremony or speeches, the great journey began.

"We took good bye of our companions," wrote McNish, "& set sail." As the *Caird* cast off the painter from the *Wills,* the men on shore gave three enthusiastic cheers.

Standing high on the beach with his small pocket camera, Hurley captured the moment of departure—the waving of caps, the uplifted arms, the brave farewell. Before he left, Shackleton, ever the entrepreneur, had given Hurley written instructions to exploit "all films & photographic reproductions" in accordance with the contracts signed before the expedition's departure.

To Frank Wild, Shackleton wrote a somewhat cryptic last letter:

April 23rd, 1916 Elephant Island

Dear Sir

In the event of my not surviving the boat journey to South Georgia you will do your best for the rescue of the party. You are in full command from the time the boat leaves this island, and all hands are under your orders. On your return to England you are to communicate with the Committee. I wish you, Lees & Hurley to write the book. You watch for my interests. In another letter you will

Hurley called this photograph "The landing on Elephant Island," but it is clear from the landscape (and identical pattern of snowfall) that this was taken on the day the Caird *was launched. In fact it depicts the* Stancomb Wills *preparing to set out on her fourth and last trip to supply the* Caird. *The object roped in the water is one of the two breakers of water for the* Caird, *which was floated in tow. The figure in the bow (facing the shore) holding the tow rope is probably Shackleton.*

The Stancomb Wills *supplying the* Caird. *"The* Wills *made heavy weather every time she came inshore, and most of the hands got wet loading her" (Wordie, Diary). Hurley called this photograph "Rescuing the Crew from Elephant Island"; but the boat is unmistakably the* Stancomb Wills, *and the photograph part of the sequence of loading the* Caird.

find the terms as agreed for lecturing you to do England Great Britain & Continent. Hurley the U.S.A. I have every confidence in you and always have had, May God prosper your work and your life. You can convey my love to my people and say I tried my best.

Yours sincerely
E. H. Shackleton

Frank Wild

"The men ashore formed a pathetic group," wrote Worsley. "As long as they thought that we could see them they kept up a wonderful appearance of optimism and heartiness."

When the *Caird* had gone, the men turned back to their lonely camp on the wind-blasted beach; what their private thoughts were at this moment, they did not reveal even to their diaries. Wild's responsibilities were unenviable. He was in charge of the care of twenty-one demoralized, partially incapacitated, and perhaps rebellious men, with one man, Blackborow, gravely ill. The deserted, barren rock on which they would have to live was, as they had slowly come to realize, daily raked by gale-force winds and blizzards. They had insufficient clothing and no shelter. They had no source of food or fuel except for penguins and seals, which could not be counted on to be around forever. They were well beyond all shipping lanes. If the *James Caird* was unsuccessful, there was, as Shackleton himself wrote, "no chance at all of any search being made . . . on Elephant Island."

South Georgia Island

"The outlook was disappointing. I looked down a sheer precipice to a chaos of crumpled ice 1,500 feet below." (Shackleton, *South*)

The Voyage of the <u>James Caird</u>

Tues 25th Fine WSW breeze running all day sky overcast.

Wed 26th W.SW gale squally & cloudy run 105 mile

Thurs 27th Northerly gale overcast & heavy squalls hove too.

Friday 28th Light N.W to W winds misty high NW swell

Sat 29th Fresh W to SW breeze sqaly running high seas

Sunday 30th hove too at 8 AM & put out sea anchor at 3 PM heavy sprays breaking
    over the boat & freezing solid.

Mon May Ist SSW gale laying to sea anchor & mizzen

Tues May 2nd—

—HENRY MCNISH, *diary*

"The tale of the next sixteen days is one of supreme strife amid heaving waters," wrote Shackleton. The crew of the *Caird* had departed on a day of rare sunshine that made the water sparkle and dance, and the peaks and glacial slopes of Elephant Island glittered with deceptive beauty as they slowly fell away behind the boat. An hour and a half after taking leave of the line of dark figures on the lonely beach, the *Caird*'s crew ran into their old enemy, the pack. Once again, they entered the eerie landscape of fantastically shaped ancient, wrecked bergs. A channel they had spotted before departure from the beach led them through the heaving, strangely rustling pack to open water by nightfall. Even on this first, relatively easy day the *Caird* shipped water, soaked by spray and soused by breaking waves. The crew wore woolen underwear under ordinary cloth trousers, Jaeger sweaters, woolen socks, mitts, and balaclavas. Over these, each man had his Burberry overalls and helmet.

"These, although windproof, were unfortunately not waterproof," Worsley observed.

Shackleton hoped to run north for a few days, away from the ice and towards warmer weather, before bearing east and setting a course for South Georgia Island. This was not the nearest landfall—Cape Horn was closer—but the prevailing westerly gales made it the only one feasible.

The men took their first meal under the low canvas deck in a heavy swell, fighting to steady the little Primus stove on which hot food depended. Unable to sit upright, they ate with great difficulty, their chests almost pressed against their stomachs. The staple of their diet was "hoosh," a brick of beef protein, lard, oatmeal, sugar, and salt originally intended as sledging rations for the transcontinental trek that now lay on the fringe of memory. Mixed with water, hoosh made a thick stew over which the coveted Nut Food could be crumbled. All but Worsley and McCarthy were seasick. After the meal, McNish, Crean, McCarthy, and Vincent crawled into their wet bags and lay down on the hard, shifting ballast of stones, while Worsley and Shackleton shared the first watch. With the Southern Cross shining from the clear, cold sky overhead, they sailed north by the stars.

"Do you know I know nothing about boat-sailing?" Worsley reports Shackleton as saying with a laugh, on this first night watch. He continues: "'Alright, Boss,' I replied, 'I do, this is my third boat-journey.'"

Worsley's report of the conversation was intended as a tribute to Shackleton's courage in undertaking such a dangerous voyage as a land explorer whose seafaring days were behind him. But in fact, it is striking how many of the British polar explorers were experienced sailors. Not only had Shackleton served twenty years in the Merchant Service, but each member of the *James Caird*'s small crew had so many years of experience at sea that expertise was taken for granted. Each man had the assurance that when he went "below deck" to crawl into his bag, his companions above who worked the sails and tiller knew, even under the unprecedented conditions, exactly what they were doing.

By dawn, when Crean emerged to light the Primus, the *Caird* had made forty-five miles from Elephant Island. Breakfast was prepared below deck, with the sea breaking over the canvas covering and running down the men's necks. In the afternoon, the wind rose to a gale from the west-southwest, with a dangerous high cross sea that racked the heavily ballasted boat with a hard, jerky motion. Shackleton divided the crew into two watches, with himself, Crean, and McNish taking one, and Worsley, McCarthy, and Vincent the other, rotating four-hour shifts.

"The routine," wrote Worsley, "was, three men in bags deluding themselves that they were sleeping, and three men 'on deck'; that is one man steering for an hour, while the other two when not pumping, baling or handling sails were sitting in our 'saloon' (the biggest part of the boat, where we generally had grub)." Going "below" was a dreaded ordeal: The space amid the increasingly waterlogged ballast was only five by seven feet. The men had to line up one behind the other and crawl, in heavy, wet clothes, over the stones and under a low thwart to reach their bags. With the boat rolling and shipping water, entrapment in this narrow space held all the horror of being buried alive, and many times men who had nodded off awoke to the sickening sensation that they were drowning.

"Real rest we had none," wrote Shackleton. The worn-out reindeer-skin bags were shedding badly, and their bristly hairs appeared everywhere—in the men's clothes, in their food, in their mouths. There was nothing to relieve the long hours of darkness, from six at night until seven in the morning; the boat carried only a makeshift oil lamp and two candles, which provided meager, carefully hoarded light. On the first night out, the cries of penguins coming from the dark sea reminded the men of lost souls.

On the third day, despite snowy, stormy weather, Worsley snatched the journey's first observation of the sun between patches of racing cloud. Kneeling on a thwart while Vincent and McCarthy strained to brace him in the pitching boat, Worsley managed to fix his sextant and take his "snap." The precious almanac and logarithm charts, against which the observations were calculated, had become dangerously pulpy, the pages sticking together and the numbers blurred. Nonetheless, Worsley's calculations revealed that they had come 128 miles from Elephant Island.

They were, however, widely off the position he had previously reckoned. Worsley wrote,

> Navigation is an art, but words fail to give my efforts a correct name. Dead reckoning or DR—the seaman's calculation of courses and distance—had become a merry jest of guesswork. . . . The procedure was: I peered out from our burrow—precious sextant cuddled under my chest to prevent seas falling on it. Sir Ernest stood by under the canvas with chronometer pencil and book. I shouted "Stand by," and knelt on the thwart—two men holding me up on either side. I brought the sun down to where the horizon ought to be and as the boat leaped frantically upward on the crest of a wave, snapped a good guess at the altitude and yelled, "Stop," Sir Ernest took the time, and I worked out the result. . . . My navigation books had to be half opened page by page till the right one was reached, then opened carefully to prevent utter destruction.

Steering at night was especially difficult. Under dense skies that allowed no light from moon or stars, the boat charged headlong into the darkness, the men steering by the "feel" of the wind, or the direction of a small pennant attached to the mast. Once or twice each night, the wind direction was verified by compass, lit by a single precious match. And yet navigation was every bit as critical as keeping the boat upright; the men knew that even a mile off course could result in a missed landfall, and the *Caird* would be swept into 3,000 miles of ocean.

In the afternoon of the third day, the gale backed to the north, and then blew continuously the next twenty-four hours. The heaving waves were gray, the sky and lowering clouds were gray, and all was obscured with mist. Heavy seas poured over the *Caird*'s port quarter. The canvas decking, sagging under the weight of so much water, threatened to pull loose the short nails McNish had extracted from packing cases. As if to underscore their own vulnerability, a flotsam of ship wreckage drove past them.

"We were getting soaked on an average every three or four minutes," wrote Worsley. "This went on day and night. The cold was intense." Particularly hateful was the task of working the pump, which one man had to hold hard against the bottom of the boat with bare hands—a position that could not be endured beyond five or six minutes at a time.

In the afternoon of April 28, the fifth day, the wind died and the seas settled into the towering swells characteristic of the latitude; "The highest, broadest and longest swells in the world," as Worsley wrote. So high were the waves that the *Caird*'s sails slackened in the artificial calm between wave crests; then the little craft was lifted onto the next hill of water, and hurled down an ever-steepening slope. On the following day, a west-southwest gale pitched and rolled the *Caird* in a high lumpy sea, but gave an excellent run of ninety-two miles on the desired northeast course. They had now come 238 miles from Elephant Island, "but not in a straight line," as Worsley observed ruefully.

On April 30, the gale strengthened and shifted from the south, blowing off the ice fields behind them, as they knew by the increasing cold. Shackleton wanted to run before the wind, but realizing that the *Caird* was in danger of being swung broadside to the surging waves, or driven headlong into the sea, he reluctantly gave the order to head into the wind and stand by.

"We put out a sea anchor to keep the *James Caird*'s head up into the sea," Shackleton wrote. "This anchor consisted of a triangular canvas bag fastened to the end of the painter and allowed to stream out from the bows." The drag of the sea anchor counteracted the boat's drift to the lee, and held her head into the wind so that she met the sea head-on. Up until now, however much the *Caird* was battered, however much icy water she shipped, she had moved forward, slowly, perceptibly closing the distance that lay between them and South Georgia. Now, soaked by bitter spray, the men waited anxiously in the pitching darkness and knew their suffering brought little progress.

"Looking out abeam," wrote Shackleton, "we would see a hollow like a tunnel formed as the crest of a big wave toppled over on to the swelling body of water." The spray that broke upon the reeling boat froze almost on impact, and towards the end of the eighth day, the *Caird*'s motion had changed alarmingly. No longer rising with the swell of the sea, she hung leaden in the water. Every soaking inch of wood, canvas, and line had frozen solid. Encased in icy armor fifteen inches thick, she was sinking like a dead weight.

Immediate action had to be taken. While the wind howled and the sea shattered over them, the men took turns crawling across the precariously glassy deck to chip away the ice. Worsley tried to evoke the unimaginable "difficulty and the peril of that climb in the darkness up that fragile slippery bit of decking. . . . Once, as the boat gave a tremendous lurch, I saw Vincent slide right across the icy sheathing of the canvas. . . . Fortunately he managed to grasp the mast just as he was going overboard."

Three times the boat had to be chipped clear. Whether using an axe or a knife, the task required strength, but also delicacy as the canvas decking had to be protected from damage at all cost. Flimsy though it was, it was their only shelter, and without it they could not survive. Two of the hated sleeping bags were now discarded; they had frozen solid in the night and had previously begun to putrefy—Shackleton estimated that they weighed as much as forty pounds apiece. By these painstaking efforts, the *Caird* rose incrementally in the water and began to rise and fall again with the movement of the swell.

The next morning, the *Caird* gave a sudden, sickening roll leeward; the painter carrying the sea anchor had been severed by a block of ice that had formed on it, out of reach. Beating the ice off the canvas, the men scrambled to unfurl the frozen sails, and once they succeeded in raising them, headed the *Caird* into the wind. It was on this day, May 2, that McNish abruptly gave up any attempt to keep a diary.

"We held the boat up to the gale during that day, enduring as best we could discomforts that amounted to pain," wrote Shackleton, in an uncharacteristically direct reference to their physical suffering. The men were soaked to the bone and frostbitten. They were badly chafed by wet clothes that had not been removed for seven months, and afflicted with saltwater boils. Their wet feet and legs were a sickly white color and swollen. Their hands were black—with grime, blubber, burns from the Primus and frostbite. The least movement was excruciating.

"We sat as still as possible," wrote Worsley. "[I]f we moved a quarter of an inch one way or the other we felt cold, wet garments on our flanks and sides. Sitting very still for a while, life was worth living." Hot meals afforded the only relief. Shackleton ensured that the men had hot food every four hours during the day and scalding powdered milk every four hours of the long night watches.

"Two of the party at least were very close to death," Worsley wrote. "Indeed, it might be said that [Shackleton] kept a finger on each man's pulse. Whenever he noticed that a man seemed extra cold and shivered, he would immediately order another hot drink of milk to be prepared and served to all. He never let the man know that it was on his account, lest he became nervous about himself." To stave off cold, they also drank the blubber oil that had been intended to calm the troubled seas. As Worsley noted, the oil would have sufficed for only one gale; there were ten days of gales on the journey.

Their ordeal had already taken a heavy toll on Vincent, who from late April, to use Shackleton's enigmatic words, had "ceased to be an active member of the crew." Worsley attributed the trouble to rheumatism, but the collapse appears to have been mental as much as physical, for later in the journey he does not appear to have been entirely incapacitated. Physically, he had been the strongest member of the entire *Endurance* company.

McCarthy shamed them all.

"[He] is the most irrepressible optimist I've ever met," Worsley wrote in his navigating book. "When I relieve him at the helm, boat iced & seas pourg: down yr neck, he informs me with a happy grin 'It's a grand day, sir.'"

Between Shackleton and Crean was a special rapport. As Worsley wrote,

Tom Crean had been so long and done so much with Sir E that he had become a priviledged retainer. As they turned in, a kind of wordless rumbling, muttering, growling noise could be heard issuing from the dark & gloomy lair in the bows sometimes directed at one another, sometimes at things in general, & sometimes at nothing at all. At times they were so full of quaint conceits & Crean's remarks were so Irish that I ran risk of explosion by suppressed laughter. "Go to sleep Crean & don't be clucking like an old hen." "Boss I can't eat those reindeer hairs. I'll have an inside on me like a billygoats neck. Let's give 'em to the Skipper & McCarthy. They never know what they're eating" & so on.

Worsley, despite the rank discomfort, was in his element. He was conscious of being in the midst of a great adventure—which had been his life's ambition. The fact that he was able to continue taking bemused stock of his shipmates is proof that he retained his sense of humor. Of McNish, there is little record. Shackleton stated only, "The carpenter was suffering particularly, but he showed grit and spirit." McNish appears to have endured each day's developments with his customary dour, matter-of-fact forbearance; he had not been born to a life that had promised things to be easy. Shackleton himself was in extreme discomfort; on top of everything else, his sciatica had returned.

At midnight on May 2, Shackleton relieved Worsley at the helm just as he was being struck full in the face by a torrent of water. The gale had been gaining strength for eight hours, and a heavy cross sea was running under snow squalls.

Alone at the helm, Shackleton noticed a line of clear sky behind them, and called out to the men below that it was at last clearing.

"Then a moment later I realized that what I had seen was not a rift in the clouds but the white crest of an enormous wave," wrote Shackleton. "During twenty-six years' experience of the ocean in all its moods I had not encountered a wave so gigantic. It was a mighty upheaval of the ocean, a thing quite apart from the big white-capped seas that had been our tireless enemies for so many days. I shouted, 'For God's sake, hold on! It's got us!'"

After an unnatural lull, a torrent of thundering foam broke over them. Staggering under the flood, the boat nonetheless rose, emerging, to use Shackleton's words, "half-full of water, sagging to the dead weight and shuddering under the blow." The men bailed with all their energy until they felt the *Caird* float true beneath them. Then it took a full hour of bailing to clear her.

On the morning of May 3, after blowing for forty-eight hours at its height, this fierce, bitter gale at last subsided, and the sun appeared amid great, clean cumulus clouds. The sails were unreefed, and the wet sleeping bags and clothing were hung from the mast and the deck, as they set course for South Georgia Island. It was still clear and bright at noon, enabling Worsley to take a sighting for their latitude; they had been six days without taking an observation. His calculations revealed that despite the monstrous difficulties, they had covered 444 miles since leaving Elephant Island—more than half the required distance. Suddenly, success seemed possible.

The good weather held, affording them "a day's grace," as Worsley said. On May 5, the twelfth day at sea, the *Caird* made an excellent run of ninety-six miles—the best of the journey—in lumpy swell that raked the boat. Willis Island, off the western tip of South Georgia, was 155 miles away. On May 6, a return of heavy seas and a northwest gale caused them to lay to again, with a reefed jib sail. The next day, the gale moderated, and they set course once more.

Worsley was now increasingly worried about getting his observational sights for their position. Since leaving Elephant Island fourteen days earlier, he had been able to sight the sun only four times. "Two of these," he noted, were "mere snaps or guesses through slight rifts in the clouds." He continued:

It was misty, the boat was jumping like a flea, shipping seas fore and aft and there was no "limb" to the sun so I had to observe the centre by guesswork. Astronomically, the limb is the edge of sun or moon. If blurred by cloud or fog it cannot be accurately "brought down" to the horizon. The centre is the spot required, so when the limb is too blurred you bring the centre of the bright spot behind the clouds down to the horizon. By practice and taking a series of "sights" you can obtain an average that has no bigger error than one minute of arc.

When Worsley informed Shackleton that he "could not be sure of our position to ten miles," it was decided that they would aim for the west coast of South Georgia, which was uninhabited, rather than the east coast where the whaling stations—and rescue—lay. This ensured that if they missed their landfall, the prevailing westerlies would carry them towards the other side of the island. Were they to fail to make an eastern landfall directly, the westerlies would carry them out to sea. If Worsley's calculations were correct, the *James Caird* was now a little more than eighty miles from South Georgia Island.

Before darkness fell on May 7, a piece of kelp floated by. With mounting excitement the crew sailed east-northeast through the night, and at dawn on the fifteenth day, they spotted seaweed. The thrill of anticipation made them momentarily forget the most recent setback: One of the kegs of water was discovered to have become brackish from seawater that evidently had got in when the *Caird* had almost capsized shortly before leaving Elephant Island. They were now plagued with mounting thirst.

Cape pigeons such as they had admired so many months before at Grytviken made frequent appearances, along with mollyhawks and other birds whose presence hinted at land. Worsley continued anxiously to monitor the sky, but heavy fog obscured the sun, and all else that might lie ahead. Two cormorants were spotted, birds known not to venture much beyond fifteen miles from land. There were heavy, lumpy cross swells, and when the fog cleared around noon low, hard-driving clouds bore in from the west-northwest, with misty squalls. Then at half past noon, McCarthy cried out that he saw land.

"There, right ahead through a rift in the flying scud our glad but salt-rimmed eyes saw a towering black crag with a lacework of snow around its flank," wrote Worsley. "One glimpse, and it was hidden again. We looked at each other with cheerful foolish grins. The thoughts uppermost were 'We've done it.'" The land, Cape Demidov, was only ten miles distant, and it was on course with Worsley's calculations.

By three in the afternoon, the men were staring at patches of green tussock grass that showed through the snow on the land ahead—the first living vegetation they had beheld since December 5, 1914, seventeen months before. It was impossible to make for the whaling stations: The nearest lay 150 miles away—a formidable distance given the conditions and changing winds. Also, they had been without fresh water for forty-eight hours. Two alternative landing sites were considered: Wilson Harbor, which lay north, but to windward, and was thus impossible to reach; and King Haakon Sound, which opened to the west, and where a westerly swell shattered on jagged reefs, spouting surf up to forty feet in the air.

"Our need of water and rest was wellnigh desperate," wrote Shackleton, "but to have attempted a landing at that time would have been suicidal. There was nothing for it but to haul off till the following morning." As he well knew, making landfall could be the most dangerous part of sailing.

A stormy sunset closed the day, and the men prepared to wait out the hours of darkness. Although they were weak in the extreme, their swollen mouths and burning thirst made eating almost impossible. The small crew tacked through the darkness until midnight, when they stood to, eighteen miles offshore. Then, in the bleak, early hours of the morning, the wind strengthened and, as the *Caird* rose and fell, increased to a gale that showered sleet and hail upon the men. Although they hove to with only a reefed jib, they were shipping water and forced to bail continuously. By break of day, the *Caird* was trapped in a perilously heavy cross sea and enormous swell that was driving them towards the coast.

Rain, hail, sleet, and snow hammered down, and by noon the gale had become a full-fledged hurricane whipping a mountainous sea into foam and obscuring every trace of land.

"None of us had ever seen anything like it before," wrote Worsley. The storm, he continued, "was driving us, harder than ever, straight for that ironbound coast. We thought but did not say those words, so fateful to the seaman, 'a lee shore.'"

At one in the afternoon, the clouds rent, suddenly exposing a precipitous front to their lee. The roar of breakers told them they were heading dead for unseen cliffs. In desperation, Shackleton ordered the double-reefed sails set for an attempt to beat into wind and pull away from the deadly course.

"The mainsail, reefed to a rag, was already set," wrote Worsley, "and in spite of the smallness of the reefed jib and mizzen it was the devil's own job to set them. Usually such work is completed inside of ten minutes. It took us an hour."

As the *James Caird* clawed her way against the wind, she struck each heaving swell with a brutal thud. With each blow, her bow planks opened, and water squirted in; caulked with oil paints and seal blood, the *Caird* was straining every joint. Five men pumped and bailed, while the sixth held her on her fearful course. She was not so much inching forward as being squeezed sideways.

"At intervals we lied, saying 'I think she'll clear it,'" Worsley wrote. After three hours of this battle, the land had safely receded, when suddenly the snow-covered mountains of Annenkov Island loomed out of the dusk to their lee. They had fought their way past one danger only to be blown into the path of another.

"I remember my thoughts clearly," wrote Worsley. "Regret for having brought my diary and annoyance that no one would ever know we had got so far."

"I think most of us had a feeling that the end was very near," wrote Shackleton. It was growing dark as the *Caird* floundered into the backwash of waves breaking against the island's precipitous coastline. Suddenly the wind veered round to the southwest. Coming about in the foaming, confused current, the *Caird* sheered away from the cliffs, and from destruction. Darkness fell, and the hurricane they had fought for nine hours abated.

"We stood offshore again, tired almost to the point of apathy," wrote Shackleton. "The night wore on. We were very tired. We longed for day."

When the morning of May 10 dawned, there was virtually no wind at all, but a heavy cross sea. After breakfast, chewed with great difficulty through parched lips, the men steered the *Caird* towards King Haakon Bay. The few charts at their disposal had been discovered to be incomplete or faulty, and they were guided in part by Worsley's instinct for the lay of the land.

Setting course for the bay, they approached a jagged reef line, which, in Shackleton's words, seemed "like blackened teeth" to bar entrance to the inlet. As they steered towards what appeared to be a propitious gap, the wind shifted once again, blowing right out of the bay, against them. Unable to approach directly, they backed off and tried to tack in, angling for entry. Five times they bore up and tacked, and on the last attempt the *Caird* sailed through the gap and into the mouth of the bay.

It was nearly dusk. A small cove guarded by a reef appeared to the south. Standing in the bows, Shackleton directed the boat through a narrow entrance in the reef.

"In a minute or two we were inside," wrote Shackleton, "and in the gathering darkness the *James Caird* ran in on a swell and touched the beach."

Jumping out, he held the frayed painter and pulled against the backward surge; and when the boat rolled in again with the surf, the other men stumbled ashore and loosely secured her. The sound of running water drew them to a small stream nearly at their feet. They fell upon their knees and drank their fill.

"It was," wrote Shackleton, "a splendid moment."

McNish's handiwork had stood up to all that the elements had flung at it. Throughout their seventeen-day ordeal, Worsley had never allowed his mind to relax and cease its calculations. Together, the six men had maintained a ship routine, a structure of command, a schedule of watches. They had been mindful of their seamanship under the most severe circumstances a sailor would ever face. They had not merely endured; they had exhibited the grace of expertise under ungodly pressure.

Undoubtedly they were conscious of having achieved a great journey. They would later learn that a 500-ton steamer had foundered with all hands in the same hurricane they had just weathered. But at the moment they could hardly have known—or cared—that in the carefully weighed judgment of authorities yet to come, the voyage of the *James Caird* would be ranked as one of the greatest boat journeys ever accomplished.

South Georgia Island

Looking into the uncharted interior of the island.

South Georgia Island

Struggling through the surf on shaky legs, the men unloaded the stores and gear and much of the ballast in order to bring the *Caird* onto land. But to no effect. Even when the boat was virtually empty, they found that their combined strength could not budge her.

"We were all about done up," wrote McNish, who had resumed his diary. "We left her rolling in the surf for the night with 1 man on watch." Shackleton had spotted a cave on one side of the cove as they were running in, and into this the men staggered for the night. While the others tried to sleep in their wet clothes and four wet bags, Shackleton took the first watch, calling Crean out at 1 a.m. when he felt himself dropping asleep on his feet. It was a difficult job, holding the *Caird* by its short, frayed painter as it rolled in the surf in the darkness. At 3 a.m., she broke free from Crean, and all hands had to be awakened to pull her back. The men were so exhausted that they could not even turn the boat over in order to roll her up the beach, but had to stand by until daylight.

In the morning, McNish removed the strakes and upper decking in order to lighten the boat further, and with great exertion they dragged her up above the high-water mark. Now at last they could rest; without the *Caird* they would have been lost as there was no way out of the cove except by sea.

King Haakon Bay was a deep sound flanked to the north and south by steep, glacier-streaked mountains. Their cave was in a recess of overhanging cliff at the back of the small cove they had entered, on the bay's southern headland. At the foot of the mountains grew clumps of rough tussock grass, which the men strewed on the floor of the cave. Huge icicles that hung like curtains at the cave mouth provided a windbreak, protecting the fire they had lit with driftwood.

Shackleton and Crean went prospecting up a slope covered with tussock grass above the beach and returned with fledgling albatrosses they had found in scattered nests. Four birds of about fourteen pounds apiece went into the hoosh pot, with Bovril rations added for thickening.

"The flesh was white and succulent, and the bones, not fully formed, almost melted in our mouths," wrote Shackleton. "That was a memorable meal." Afterward, they lay in their bags drying tobacco in the fire embers and smoking.

"We have not been as comfortable for the last 5 weeks," wrote McNish with satisfaction. "We had 3 young & 1 old albatross for lunch with 1 pint of gravy which beets all the chicken soup I ever tasted. I have just been thinking what our companions would say if they had food like this."

On the day after arriving in the cove, Shackleton had already announced the next stage of the rescue. Stromness Bay, where the nearest manned whaling stations lay, was about 150 miles distant by sea. But given the treacherous weather and coastline, it was simply too far for the battered boat and debilitated crew to attempt; there would be no more boat journeys. Instead, Shackleton decided that he and two others would cross overland to one of the several stations at Stromness, a distance of about twenty-two miles—twenty-two miles as the crow flies, that is. Actually, there was no such thing as a straightforward journey across South Georgia Island. Although the highest mountains on the island were just under 10,000 feet, the interior was a confusion of jagged rocky upthrusts and treacherous crevasses, overlain with deep snow and thick ice. To further complicate matters, no one had ever made this crossing before. No maps existed to guide the way.

"We had very scanty knowledge of the conditions of the interior," wrote Shackleton. "No man had ever penetrated a mile from the coast of South Georgia at any point, and the whalers I knew regarded the country as inaccessible." On the blueprint map the men carried with them the interior was depicted with a blank.

Shackleton allowed the men four days to dry, rest, sleep, and eat. They were not only exhausted and shaky from exposure, but with superficial frostbite and chafed legs, they were also in some pain. Mentally, too, no one had entirely recovered from the journey. On the night of May 12, according to Worsley, Shackleton suddenly "awoke us all by loudly shouting: 'Look out, boys, look out!'" He had been dreaming of the great wave that had come so close to engulfing them.

Yet for all their fatigue, two days after landing, Shackleton, Worsley, and Crean were out scouting the land, and McNish was back at work repairing the *Caird*. Access to the island's interior could be gained only from the head of the bay, where a pass led through the mountains. In turn, the head of the bay could be reached only by boat.

"I am still busy at the boat," wrote McNish. "While the skipper does the Nimrod

& bring home the food Vincent lays down by the fire & smoks some times coming out for more wood while the Boss & Creen looks after the cooking & McCarthy is my assistant. We had four young birds for lunch then we think of hard times."

On the day before they left the haven of their cove, McNish went for a walk.

"I went on top of the hill & had a lay on the grass & it put me in mind of old times at *Home* sitting on the hillside looking down at the sea."

This last day also brought them an unexpectedly good omen. The rudder of the *Caird* had been lost during the landing; now, while McCarthy stood by the water line, the same rudder, as Shackleton wrote, "with all the broad Atlantic to sail in and the coasts of two continents to search for a resting-place, came bobbing back into our cove."

May 15 dawned with a gusty northwesterly wind and misty showers of rain. After breakfast at 7:30 a.m., the men loaded up the *Caird* and, navigating through the cove's narrow entrance, sailed forth into the bay. The sun came out briefly, and although the sea was running high the crew were all in good spirits. Approaching the north shore just after noon, they could hear the roar of sea elephants, and soon the *Caird* landed on a sandy beach amid hundreds of the animals.

The weather had turned again, and in a fine, drizzling rain, the men dragged the boat above the high-water mark and turned it over so as to form a shelter. With one side set up on stones to make an entrance and the whole covered over with turf, the *Caird* made a snug enough hut, and was nicknamed Peggotty Camp, after Dickens's boat hut of the same name. A sea elephant provided them with food and fuel for the night. Scattered close by over half an acre was a litter of driftwood—masts, bits of figureheads, brass caps, broken oars, timbers—"a graveyard of ships," as Worsley noted. When the moon came out, Crean yelled that he had seen a rat.

"We jeered at him," said Worsley, "and with tears in my voice I implored him to give me a little of what had made him see rats; but when, some time later, the carpenter also thought he saw one, our derision was less pronounced." They concluded the rats had come ashore with the wreckage.

Bad weather, with snow and hail, kept them more or less in their new shelter for the next three days, with Shackleton becoming increasingly restless. Once, Shackleton and Worsley ventured out to scout the pass they would take through the mountains, but they were driven back by a sudden snowstorm.

"I'll never take another expedition, Skipper," Worsley reported Shackleton saying. They were anxious to set out while the moon was still full, but could not do so without a break in the weather. Winter was settling in fast, and with it their chances were dimming.

Their moment came at 2 a.m. on May 19. With a full moon shining in a still, clear sky, Shackleton knew the conditions would never be better. He, Crean, and Worsley took their breakfast hoosh and just over an hour later began the trek. Vincent and McCarthy appear to have remained in their bags, but McNish accompanied them for the first 200 or so yards.

"He could do no more," wrote Shackleton simply. In the last blank pages of McNish's diary, Shackleton had written in a bold, confident hand a final directive:

May 16, 1916
South Georgia

Sir

I am about to try and reach Husvik on the East Coast of this island for relief for our party. I am leaving you in charge of this party consisting of Vincent, MacCarthy & yourself. You will remain here until relief arrives. You have ample seal food which you can supplement with birds & fish according to your skill. You are left with a double barrelled gun, 50 cartridges—40 to 50 Bovril sledging rations, 25 to 30 biscuits: 40 Streimers Nutfood—you also have all the necessary equipment to support life for an indefinite period. In the event of my non-return you had better after winter is over try and sail round to the East Coast. The course I am making towards Husvik is East magnetic.

I trust to have you relieved in a few days.

Yours faithfully
E. H. Shackleton

H. McNish.

As McNish returned to Peggotty Camp, the three men set out past the ship grave-yard, under moonlight that cast long shadows over the glinting mountain peaks and glaciers. They were soon ascending a snow slope that emerged just north of the head of the bay from an inland saddle between the ranges of mountains. Shackleton had originally intended to take along a small sledge, constructed by McNish, to carry sleeping bags and gear. In a trial run the day before departure, however, it had become apparent that such a conveyance was not suited to the terrain.

"After consultation we decided to leave the sleeping-bags behind and make the journey in very light marching order," wrote Shackleton. "We would take three days' provisions for each man in the form of sledging ration and biscuit. The food was to be packed in three socks, so that each member of the party could carry his own sup-ply." Additionally, they carried the Primus lamp filled with oil for six hot meals, forty-eight matches, the small hoosh pot, two compasses, a pair of binoculars, ninety feet of rope, and McNish's adze, this to be used as an ice axe. Worsley still carried the ship's chronometer around his neck. In lieu of a walking stick, each man had taken a piece of the wood from the *Caird*'s former decking. Their Jaeger woolen underwear and cloth trousers were by now threadbare.

"I was unfortunate as regarded footgear, since I had given away my heavy Burberry boots on the floe, and had now a comparatively light pair in poor condition," wrote Shackleton. "The carpenter assisted me by putting several screws in the sole of each boot with the object of providing a grip on the ice." The screws had been taken from the *James Caird*.

With Worsley as navigator, they began their ascent of the snowy uplift and soon discovered that the surface had deteriorated from the hard, packed snow of just two days before, to a soft mush that sank over their ankles with each step. After two hours, they had reached 1,000 feet, high enough to obtain a view of the coast below, and to see that their road to the interior would not take them over gentle snowfields, but formidable undulations of snow broken by treacherously steep ranges. As they slogged on up towards the saddle, a thick fog rolled in, obscuring the moon. The men roped themselves together and continued blindly through the opaque mist, with Shackleton breaking the trail, and Worsley giving directions from the rear.

At the top of the saddle, in the early dawn light, the mist thinned sufficiently to open a partial view down upon what appeared to be a frozen lake. Taking a short break to eat a biscuit, they struck out for it, as Shackleton believed that this course would be easier than keeping to the high ground. After an hour of walking, they began to notice signs of crevasses, and realized they were walking on a snow-covered glacier. They continued cautiously until the mist below cleared enough to reveal that the water was neither a lake, nor frozen, as a trick of the light had led them to believe. It was in fact Possession Bay, an arm of the sea on the eastern coast, roughly opposite their own King Haakon Bay on the west. Knowing that the coast was impassable, they had no choice but to turn back and retrace their steps. It was a foolish error, for Possession Bay was marked clearly on their map, but it gives some idea of the utter lack of context in which they had begun the march.

The sun rose in a calm, cloudless sky, promising continued, rare good weather; haste had to be made while circumstances permitted. In daylight, however, the snow surface became softer than ever, and at times they sank up to their knees, slogging along in a manner that must have evoked for Shackleton and Crean their man-hauling sledging marches of so long ago. At 9 a.m. they paused for their first meal. The hoosh pot was filled with snow, and Crean lit the Primus. When the snow was melted, two bricks of sledging rations were added, and the hoosh eaten as hot and as quickly as possible.

The march continued, with a one-minute break every quarter of an hour, which they took lying flat on their backs, spread-eagled in the snow. Since departing Patience Camp on April 9, six weeks before, the men had had little opportunity even to stretch their legs; twenty-four days of those six weeks had been spent cramped in the rocking boats. Their frostbitten feet had not yet regained all feeling, and their clothes, saturated with salt water, now rubbed their chafed inner thighs raw. Now, climbing knee deep in snow, they were quickly exhausted.

Two hours after their meal, they reached a range of five rocky crags that stood, like the stubby fingers of an upheld hand, across their path. The gaps between the crags appeared to offer four distinct passes to the land behind. Aiming for the closest and southernmost of these, Shackleton led the way, cutting steps up the slope with the adze as they drew nearer to the crest.

"The outlook was disappointing," Shackleton reported from the top. "I looked down a sheer precipice to a chaos of crumpled ice 1500 ft. below. There was no way down for us." A mountain crag prevented them from crossing over to the next pass, and so they could do nothing but retrace their steps down the long slope that had taken them three hours to climb.

Eager to make up lost ground, they began the tramp up to the second gap without ado, halting only for a hasty meal. But on reaching the "pass" they were again disappointed.

"We stood between two gigantic black crags that seemed to have forced their way upwards through their icy covering," wrote Worsley. "Before us was the Allardyce range, peak beyond peak, snow-clad and majestic, glittering in the sunshine. Sweeping down from their flanks were magnificent glaciers, noble to look upon, but, as we realized, threatening to our advance."

Wearily, numbly, they made yet another retreat down yet another slope, and pinned their hopes upon the third pass.

"Each of these successive climbs was steeper," wrote Worsley, "and this third one, which brought us to about five thousand feet above sea level, was very exhausting." They reached the top of the third gap at four in the afternoon, as the sun was beginning to set and the chill of the coming night was setting in. But the prospect below them was no better than it had been from the other gaps. As Worsley pointed out, the whole of their afternoon's labor had proved valueless. They had been on the march some thirteen hours, and were numb with fatigue. And yet lying down to rest—or giving up completely—was not something that appears to have crossed any of their minds. Shackleton knew that his two companions would never balk and never complain. They in turn knew that he would continue actively to search out and lead a way until he dropped. Through all the long, stumbling hours, they remained a tight, unflinchingly loyal unit.

Now, looking towards the most northern and last pass, a way down did appear possible. Without delay, they retraced their steps for the third time, and braced for a fourth ascent.

At the bottom of the last pass, they encountered a great chasm, some 200 feet deep, that had been carved out of the snow and ice by wind—a chilling reminder of what a gale at these heights was capable of. Carefully making their way around this, they began the ascent of a razor-back of ice that sloped up towards the last gap. At their backs, a thick fog was creeping over the land, obscuring all that lay behind them. At the top of the pass, they straddled the narrow ridge, and with wisps of rising fog lapping around them, surveyed the scene. After an initial precipitous drop, the land merged into a long, declining snow slope, the bottom of which lay hidden in mist and growing darkness.

"I don't like our position at all," Worsley quotes Shackleton as saying. With night coming on, they were in danger of freezing at this altitude. Shackleton remained silent for some minutes, thinking.

"We've got to take a risk," he said at length. "Are you game?" Throwing their legs over the ridge, they began a painstaking descent. With Shackleton cutting footholds in the snow-covered precipice, they advanced inches at a time. At the end of half an hour, the three men had covered a little more than 300 feet and reached the long snow slope. Shackleton considered their situation again. With no sleeping bags and only tattered clothes, they would not survive a night in the mountains, so halting was out of the question. The way behind them offered no hope of a route, so they could not go back. They had to continue. Urging them on, always, was the fear of a change in the weather.

"We'll slide," Worsley reports Shackleton said at last. Coiling the length of rope beneath them, the three men sat down, one behind the other, each straddling with his legs and locking his arms around the man ahead. With Shackleton in the front and Crean bringing up the rear, they pushed off towards the pool of darkness far below.

"We seemed to shoot into space," wrote Worsley. "For a moment my hair fairly stood on end. Then quite suddenly I felt a glow, and knew that I was grinning! I was actually enjoying it. . . . I yelled with excitement, and found that Shackleton and Crean were yelling too."

As their speed diminished, they knew the slope was levelling off, and they were finally brought to a gentle halt by a bank of snow. Rising to their feet, they solemnly shook hands all round. In only a few minutes, they had covered 1,500 feet.

They resumed their tramp for about half a mile across a level upland of snow, then stopped for another meal. At 7 p.m., the moon rose and spread its light over a majestic scene.

"The great snowy uplands gleamed white before us," wrote Worsley. "Enormous peaks towered awe-inspiringly round about, and to the south was the line of black crags, while northwards lay the silvered sea." Their scramble in the heights had at least given them a clearer sense of the lay of the land.

The brief meal finished, they set out again and around midnight came upon a long, welcome, sloping decline. They moved now more carefully than ever, wary, at this last stage, of putting a foot wrong.

"When men are as tired as we were," wrote Worsley, "their nerves are on edge, and it is necessary for each man to take pains not to irritate the others. On this march we treated each other with a good deal more consideration than we should have done in normal circumstances. Never is etiquette and 'good form' observed more carefully than by experienced travellers when they find themselves in a tight place."

After two hours of a relatively easy downhill trek, they found themselves approaching a bay, which they took to be Stromness. With mounting excitement they began to point out familiar landmarks, such as Blenheim Rocks, which lay off one of the whaling stations. Almost giddy with anticipation, they continued to tramp along until suddenly the appearance of crevasses told them they were on a glacier.

"I knew there was no glacier in Stromness," Shackleton recorded grimly. As at the very outset of their march, they had allowed themselves to be seduced into taking an erroneous route by the relative ease it promised. Wearily, despondently they turned back, setting a tangential course for the southeast.

They took nearly three hours to regain their former altitude at the foot of the rocky spurs of the range. It was five o'clock in the morning of May 20. Dawn was only a few hours away. A wind had begun to blow which, enervated as they were, chilled them to the bone. Shackleton ordered a brief rest, and within minutes Worsley and Crean had sunk down upon the snow and fallen asleep in each other's arms for warmth. Shackleton remained awake.

"I realized it would be disastrous if we all slumbered together," he wrote, "for sleep under such conditions merges into death. After five minutes I shook them into consciousness again, told them that they had slept for half an hour, and gave the word for a fresh start."

So stiff from the unaccustomed rest that they had to walk with their knees bent until fully warmed up, the men set course for a jagged range of peaks ahead; they were truly entering familiar territory now, and knew this range to be a ridge that ran in from Fortuna Bay, around the corner from Stromness. As they struggled up the steep slope leading to a gap in the range, they were met with a blast of icy wind. They passed over the gap just as dawn was breaking, and stopped to catch their breath.

Directly below them lay Fortuna Bay; but there, across a range of mountains to the east, they could see the distinctive, twisted rock formation that identified Stromness Bay. They stood in silence, then for the second time turned and shook hands with each other.

"To our minds the journey was over," wrote Shackleton, "though as a matter of fact twelve miles of difficult country had still to be traversed." But now they knew they would do it.

While Crean prepared breakfast with the last of their fuel, Shackleton climbed a higher ridge for a better view. At 6:30 a.m., he thought he heard the sound of a steam whistle; he knew that about this time the men at the whaling stations would be roused from bed. Scrambling down to the camp, he told the others; if he had heard correctly, another whistle should sound at seven o'clock, when the men were summoned to work. With intense excitement, the three waited, watching as the hands moved round on Worsley's chronometer; and at seven o'clock to the minute, they heard the whistle again. It was the first noise from the world of men they had heard since December 5, 1914. And it told them the station was manned; only hours away were men and ships, and with them the rescue of the company on Elephant Island.

Abandoning the Primus stove that had served them so well, they began their descent of the range, floundering down a slope of the deepest snow they had encountered during the journey. The descent steepened, and the snow gave way to blue ice. Worsley suggested returning to a safer route, but Shackleton adamantly insisted that they press ahead. They had been on the march for twenty-seven hours, and their reserves of endurance were running low. Always, there was the threat of bad weather; even now, a sudden gale or snowstorm could finish them off.

Cautiously at first, they cut steps with the adze; then, impatiently, Shackleton lay on his back and kicked footholds in the ice as he descended, while Worsley gave a pretence of supporting him by rope from his own precarious position above. In reality, a slip from Shackleton would have pulled them all down.

It took three hours to descend the short distance to the sandy beach of Fortuna Bay and a quagmire of glacial mud that sucked at their boots. Here, too, they came upon evidence of man, "whose work," as Shackleton wrote, "as is so often the case, was one of destruction." The bodies of several seals bearing bullet wounds were lying around. Bypassing these, they headed for the opposite side of the bay.

By half past noon, they had crossed the opposing slope of the bay and were working their way over a blessedly flat plateau towards the last ridge that lay between them and Stromness Station. Suddenly, Crean broke through what turned out to be ice beneath them; the "plateau" was a frozen tarn, covered with snow. Wet to his waist, he was hauled out, and the three men continued gingerly until safely ashore.

An hour later they stood on the last ridge, looking down into Stromness Bay. A whaling boat came in sight, and after it a sailing ship; tiny figures could be seen moving about the sheds of the station. For the last time on the journey, they turned and shook each other's hands.

Marching mechanically now, too tired for thought, they moved through the last stages of their trek. Searching for a way down the ridge to the harbor, they followed the course of a small stream, up to their ankles in its icy water. The stream ended in a waterfall with a twenty-five-foot drop, and without a second thought, they determined to follow it over. There was no time left, their strength and wits were failing; they could no longer calculate or strategize, but only keep moving forward. Securing one end of their worn rope to a boulder, they first lowered Crean over the edge, and he vanished entirely into the waterfall. Then Shackleton, and then Worsley, who was, as Shackleton wrote, "the lightest and most nimble of the party." Leaving the rope dangling, they staggered ahead.

At three in the afternoon, they arrived at the outskirts of Stromness Station. They had traveled for thirty-six hours without rest. Their bearded faces were black with blubber smoke, and their matted hair, clotted with salt, hung almost to their shoulders. Their filthy clothes were in tatters; in vain Worsley had tried to pin together the seat of his trousers, shredded in their glissade down the mountain. Close to the station they encountered the first humans outside their own party they had set eyes on in nearly eighteen months—two small children, who ran from them in fright. As in a dream the men kept moving, through the outskirts of the station, through the dark digesting house, out towards the wharf, each banal fixture of the grimy station now fraught with significance. A man saw them, started, and hurriedly passed on, probably thinking the ragged trio were drunken, derelict sailors—it would not have occurred to anyone that there could be castaways on South Georgia Island.

The station foreman, Matthias Andersen, was on the wharf. Speaking English, Shackleton asked to be taken to Captain Anton Andersen, who had been winter manager when the *Endurance* sailed. Looking them over, the foreman replied that Captain Andersen was no longer there, but he would take them to the new manager, Thoralf Sørlle. Shackleton nodded; he knew Sørlle. Sørlle had entertained them two years previously, when the expedition had touched in at Stromness.

Tactfully unquestioning, the foreman led the three to the station manager's home.

"Mr. Sørlle came out to the door and said, 'Well?'" Shackleton recorded.

"'Don't you know me?' I said.

"'I know your voice,' he replied doubtfully. 'You're the mate of the *Daisy.*'"

An old Norwegian whaler who was also present gave an account, in his broken English, of the meeting.

"Manager say: 'Who the *hell* are you?' and terrible bearded man in the centre of the three say very quietly: 'My name is Shackleton.' Me—I turn away and weep."

They had done it all; and now long-held dreams came true. Hot baths, the first in two years; a shave, clean new clothes, and all the cakes and starch they could eat. The hospitality of the whalers was boundless. After an enormous meal, Worsley was despatched with a relief ship, the *Samson*, to collect the rest of the party at King Haakon Bay, while Shackleton and Sørlle urgently talked over plans to rescue the men on Elephant Island.

That night, the weather took a turn for the worse. Lying in his bunk on the *Samson*, Worsley listened to the rising gale.

South Georgia Island

"In memories we were rich. We had pierced the veneer of outside things. We had 'suffered, starved and triumphed, grovelled down yet grasped at glory, grown bigger in the bigness of the whole.' We had seen God in His splendours, heard the text that Nature renders. We had reached the naked soul of man." (Shackleton, South, *describing the end of the crossing of South Georgia*)

"Had we been crossing that night," he wrote, "nothing could have saved us." McNish, McCarthy, and Vincent were sheltered under the upturned *Caird* when Worsley came ashore in a whaler to greet them the following morning. Thrilled to be rescued, they nonetheless grumbled that none of their own party had come and that collecting them had been left to the Norwegians.

"'Well, I'm here,'" Worsley reported himself as saying, clearly delighted by the turn of events.

"[T]hey stared," he continued. "Clean and shaved, they had taken me for a Norwegian!"

Taking up their meager possessions, the last of the *James Caird* crew boarded the *Samson*, McNish holding his diary. Worsley had also determined to bring the *James Caird* along. The men had none of the depth of feeling for her they had held for the *Endurance*, which had sheltered and protected them as long as she was able; nonetheless, though the *Caird* had provided them little comfort, they and she had battled for their lives together and had won.

A great gale and snowstorm descended on the *Samson* as she approached Stromness, keeping her at sea for two extra days. But mindless of the weather, the men on board ate and rested to their hearts' content.

In Sørlle's home, Shackleton and Crean lay in bed, listening to the snow drive against the windows. They now knew how slim had been their margin of safety. On Sunday, May 21, Shackleton sailed round to Husvik Station, also in Stromness Bay, to arrange a loan of a likely rescue ship, the English-owned *Southern Sky*, for immediate departure to Elephant Island. Another old friend from *Endurance* days, Captain Thom, was in the harbor and immediately signed on as captain; the whalers eagerly volunteered as crew.

When the *Samson* arrived in the harbor, the men from the whaling station came to greet her, and congregated around the *James Caird*, carrying the boat ashore on their shoulders.

"The Norwegians would not let us put a hand to her," wrote Worsley. That same night, Monday evening, Sørlle held a reception at the station clubhouse for Shackleton, and invited the captains and officers of his whaling fleet.

"They were 'old stagers,'" Shackleton recorded, "with faces lined and seamed by the storms of half a century."

The club room was "blue and hazy with tobacco smoke," according to Worsley. "Three or four white-haired veterans of the sea came forward. One spoke in Norse, and the Manager translated. He said he had been at sea over 40 years; that he knew this stormy Southern Ocean intimately, from South Georgia to Cape Horn, from Elephant Island to the South Orkneys, and that never had he heard of such a wonderful feat of daring seamanship as bringing the 22-foot open boat from Elephant Island to South Georgia. . . . All the seamen present then came forward and solemnly shook hands with us in turn. Coming from brother seamen, men of our own cloth and members of a great seafaring race like the Norwegians, this was a wonderful tribute."

Passages back to England were arranged for McNish, Vincent, and McCarthy; tensions between McNish and Vincent and the rest of the party seem to have persisted until the very end. McNish's description of Worsley doing "the Nimrod," a facetious reference to the great biblical hunter, shows that he had lost none of his fine sardonic touch in the course of the journey. Likewise, his dry observation that Vincent remained in his bag smoking while others did work suggests that Vincent's performance in the boats had not changed the carpenter's opinion of this young cub of a trawler. The attitude of Shackleton and Worsley to these two men would be made manifest much later. Together, the six had performed a prodigy of seamanship and courage; but they parted as they had entered the expedition—tough, independent-minded, unsentimental old salts. None of the three returning to England would see one another, or any member of the *James Caird* crew, ever again.

On May 23, only three days after their arrival in Stromness, Shackleton, Worsley, and Crean left in the *Southern Sky* for Elephant Island. This was the moment for which Shackleton had lived through all the difficult days. Driving steadily against the familiar westerly gales, the *Southern Sky* was within 100 miles of Elephant Island when she ran into ice. Forty miles farther, she was brought to a complete stop.

"To attempt to force the unprotected steel whaler through the masses of pack-ice that now confronted us would have been suicidal," wrote Worsley. Skirting the pack for many miles, they began to run dangerously low of coal, and were at last forced to turn back. The *Southern Sky* now made for the Falkland Islands in order to seek another vessel; from here Shackleton was able to cable to England.

News of Shackleton's survival created a sensation. Newspaper headlines heralded the story, and the king cabled the Falklands with a congratulatory message:

"Rejoice to hear of your safe arrival in the Falkland Islands and trust your companions on Elephant Island may soon be rescued.—George, R.I."

Even Robert F. Scott's widow, Kathleen Scott, ever watchful of her husband's reputation, conceded, "Shackleton or no Shackleton, I think it is one of the most wonderful adventures I ever read of, magnificent."

But for all the excitement, the British government was not able to provide for the final rescue. Britain was still at war and had no spare ships for non-military efforts, let alone any fitted for the ice. The only suitable vessel was the *Discovery*, Scott's old ship—but she could not be ready to sail before October.

This was not good enough. The Foreign Office approached the governments of

Uruguay, Argentina, and Chile for assistance as Shackleton desperately scoured the southern ports for an appropriate wooden vessel. More than anyone alive, he knew how difficult it would be to find one—the stout little *Endurance* had been unique. On June 10, the Uruguayan government came forward with a small survey ship, the *Instituto de Pesca No 1*, and crew, for no charge. After three days, she came in sight of Elephant Island, but the ice allowed her no closer. Six days after setting out, she limped back to port.

In Punta Arenas, a subscription from the British Association chartered the *Emma*, a forty-year-old schooner built of oak, and a multinational scratch crew. Setting out on July 12, they too came to within 100 miles of Elephant Island before ice and tempestuous weather turned them back.

"Some members of the scratch crew were played out by the cold and violent tossing," wrote Shackleton, with the restrained irony of a veteran of the *James Caird*. The ferocious weather kept the *Emma* three weeks at sea, and it was August 3 before she reached harbor. Back in Punta Arenas, Shackleton waged another desperate search. The unthinkable was happening: Weeks of waiting were passing into months.

"The wear and tear of this period was dreadful," wrote Worsley. "To Shackleton it was little less than maddening. Lines scored themselves on his face more deeply day by day; his thick, dark, wavy hair was becoming silver. He had not had a grey hair when we had started out to rescue our men the first time. Now, on the third journey, he was grey-haired."

He had also begun, uncharacteristically, to drink. In a photograph taken by Hurley at Ocean Camp, Shackleton sits on the ice preoccupied, but strangely debonair. But in a photograph taken of him during this period of searching for a ship, he is utterly unrecognizable. Pinched with tension, his face is that of an old man. It was now mid-August—*four months* since the departure of the *James Caird*.

From Chile, Shackleton sent yet another cable to the Admiralty, pleading for any wooden vessel. The reply stated that the *Discovery* would arrive sometime around September 20; but it also cryptically implied that the captain of the *Discovery* would be in charge of the rescue operation—Shackleton would essentially go along as a passenger and answer to him.

Incredulous, Shackleton cabled both the Admiralty and his friend and agent Ernest Perris seeking clarification.

"Impossible to reply to your question except to say unsympathetic attitude to your material welfare," Perris replied, "and customary attitude of Navy to Mercantile Marine which it seems resulted from desire of Admiralty to boom its own relief Expedition."

Among Norwegians and South Americans Shackleton had met with nothing but open-handed and open-hearted support; only in England did the concern to put him in his place exceed that for the plight of his men. Galvanized into frenetic action by this response, Shackleton begged the Chilean government to come forward once again. Knowing perhaps that honor as well as life was now at stake, they lent him the *Yelcho*, a small, steel-built tug steamer entirely unsuitable for the purpose, and on August 25, Shackleton, Crean, and Worsley set out with a Chilean crew for Elephant Island.

In a moment of introspective summing up, Shackleton at the end of his account of crossing South Georgia had written:

> When I look back at those days I have no doubt that Providence guided us, not only across those snowfields, but across the storm-white sea that separated Elephant Island from our landing-place on South Georgia. I know that during that long and racking march of thirty-six hours over the unnamed mountains and glaciers of South Georgia it seemed to me often that we were four, not three. I said nothing to my companions on the point, but afterwards Worsley said to me, "Boss, I had a curious feeling on the march that there was another person with us." Crean confessed to the same idea.

Now that they were back in the world of men, this guiding presence seemed to have fled; and the grace and strength that had brought them so far would count for nothing if, when they eventually arrived, they found even one man dead on Elephant Island.

Hut on Elephant Island

Marston and Greenstreet suggested that the two remaining boats, the Stancomb Wills *and the* Dudley
Docker, *be converted into a hut. The boats were overturned on stone walls standing some four feet high,
and in this shelter the 22 men lived for the next four months. The remains of the tents were used for
the windbreaking "skirt" around the walls.*

Elephant Island

"We gave them three hearty cheers & watched the boat getting smaller & smaller in the distance," wrote Wild, on the departure of the *James Caird*. "Then seeing some of the party in tears I immediately set them all to work. My own heart was very full. I heard one of the few pessimists remark, 'that's the last of them' & I almost knocked him down with a rock, but satisfied myself by addressing a few remarks to him in real lower deck language."

The *Caird* had left at 12:30 p.m., and at 4:00 p.m., Wild climbed a rocky lookout from where, through binoculars, he caught the boat just before she vanished into the pack.

All hands had gotten completely or partially soaked in the process of preparing and loading the *Caird*, and after a hot lunch, everyone wrung out his sleeping bag as well as he could and went to bed for the rest of the day.

On the following morning the bay was filled with pack ice—the *Caird* had not left a day too soon. After breakfast, Wild addressed the entire company, "concisely yet pertinently relative to future attitudes," according to Hurley's approving report. Although Shackleton had gone, Wild made it clear that there was still a boss in charge. The men were put to work skinning penguins and carving out shelters in the snow. High hopes had been pinned on these snow "caves," before the men discovered that their body heat raised the temperature inside to the melting point, making things wetter than ever.

The land at their disposal was a narrow, rocky spit that jutted out from the precipitous mainland by some 600 to 700 feet. Standing about 9 feet above high tide, it was little more than 100 feet wide. A glacier to the west frequently calved enormous chunks of ice. To the east lay a narrow gravel beach used by seals and penguins. Their spit was utterly exposed to the elements.

"We pray that the *Caird* may reach South Georgia safely and bring relief without delay," wrote Hurley, still one of the toughest and most resilient members of the group. "Life here without a hut & equipment is almost beyond endurance." It was the last day of April; the *Caird* had been gone only six days.

Marston and Greenstreet suggested building a shelter using the only materials at hand: the two overturned boats. This meant taking them permanently out of commission; the stores at Cape Valentine would now be retrieved only if a second boat journey was made in the spring, in the event of the failure of the *James Caird*. Such an eventuality was unthinkable, and the need for shelter was immediate.

"Owing to the lack of carbohydrates in our diet we are all terribly weak," wrote Lees, "and this part of the work was exceedingly laborious & took us more than twice as long as it would have done had we been in normal health." Eventually, two walls standing four feet in height, nineteen feet apart were erected between two large boulders that acted as additional windbreaks. The *Stancomb Wills* and *Dudley Docker* were lain on top of the walls and weighed down with loose rocks. Odd pieces of salvaged timber were placed like rafters on top of the boats and then the whole construction was overspread with one of the large tents. More tent material was cut for outer walls, and the sack mouth entrance from one of the domed tents was attached as a doorway.

When the "Snuggery" was completed, Wild officiated over the distribution of berths. Ten men, including all the sailors, took upper "bunks" on the thwarts of the boats, while the rest were carefully arranged along the ground. The hut floor had been cleared as well as possible, but under the various remnants of ground cloths and tents there still lay ice and frozen guano. During the first night, a screaming blizzard revealed the hut's every weakness. The men had gone to bed in the weary hope that they had at last secured shelter, but they awoke to find themselves under several inches of drift.

"And then what a miserable getting up," wrote Macklin. "Everything deeply snowed over, footgear frozen so stiff that we could only put it on by degrees, not a dry or warm pair of gloves amongst us. I think I spent this morning the most unhappy hour of my life—all attempts seemed so hopeless, and Fate seemed absolutely determined to thwart us. Men sat and cursed, not loudly but with an intenseness that shewed their hatred of this island on which we had sought shelter."

But Wild persisted, and gradually the cracks through which snow and wind infiltrated were discovered and assiduously caulked with the remains of an old Jaeger woolen sleeping bag. Later, Hurley brought in a small blubber stove, which was placed in the triangle between the sterns of the two boats.

"From now on we shall always be black with smoke, but we hope, at least dry," wrote Wordie. Additional refinements, made through trial and error, increased the general comfort. A chimney constructed by Kerr from the lining of a biscuit tin removed much of the smoke, while Marston and Hurley devised blubber lamps from sardine tins, capable of shedding light for a few feet around. Hurley and Greenstreet supervised the construction of a galley, built of a six-foot-high roughly circular wall of stones, covered with the sail of the *Dudley Docker*. An oar serving as the camp's flagpole added the final touch; from it they optimistically hung the Royal Thames Yacht Club burgee.

Wild set a strict camp routine. Poor Green was roused from his bed atop some of the supply cases at 7 a.m., just before daylight. Out in the gray dawn, he made his way to the galley, where he lit the blubber stove and spent the next two to three hours preparing thick seal steaks. At 9:30 a.m., Wild turned everyone out with the

In front of hut on Elephant Island

Frank Hurley rests against the "Snuggery." "[The hut] is a decided improvement & a step in the direction of making life more endurable under such severe climatic conditions. The entire party of 22 sleep in this small space snugly though sardiniously." (Hurley, diary)

Skinning penguins. "With the little stock of seal meat and the provisions we already have one penguin per day between every two men would be quite sufficient. That is eleven penguins per day for the whole party or a total of about 1300 birds for the period May-August inclusive. At present we are merely living from hand to mouth and have as yet only a very small reserve."

(Lees, diary)

cry, "Lash up and stow! The Boss may come today." With this, the men rolled up their bags and stashed them away amid the thwarts of the boats. After breakfast, fifteen minutes was allowed for "Smoke Oh" while Wild assigned the day's various tasks—hunting, skinning, and preparing penguins and seals, shoring up the Snuggery, mending, and so forth. "Hoosh Oh" was at 12:30 p.m., and the afternoon was passed in more of the same occupations as the morning. The evening meal of seal hoosh was served at 4:30 p.m., after which everyone settled in a circle on crates placed around the bogie stove. A strict seating rotation ensured that everyone got a place close to the stove once a week.

"It is a weird sight," wrote Hurley. "The light thrown up by the lamp illuminates smoke colored faces like stage footlights. The sparkling eyes & glint on the aluminium mugs, the stream of flickering light thrown out from the open bogie door, making weird dancing shadows on the inside of the boats makes me think of a council of brigands holding revelry after an escape in a chimney or coalmine."

After "Smoke Oh," the box seats were stowed so as to form Green's bed—a concession to the fact that his Jaeger woolen bag was soaked more than most. Those in the upper berths swung up between the thwarts with practiced agility, while the others spread their groundsheets and bags. Hussey often closed out the evening with half an hour's singing and playing on his banjo. Muttered conversations continued until sleep came, around seven o'clock. During the night, sheets of ice up to half an inch thick formed along the walls from condensation of their breath.

On May 10, Hurley took a group photograph with his small pocket camera. "The most motley & unkempt assembly that ever was projected on a plate," he

The Party Marooned on Elephant Island

Hurley took this group portrait on May 10, 1916: "The most motley & unkempt assembly that ever was projected on a plate" (Hurley, diary). Back row: Greenstreet, McIlroy, Marston, Wordie, James, Holness, Hudson, Stephenson, McLeod, Clark, Lees, Kerr, Macklin. Second row: Green, Wild, How, Cheetham, Hussey, Bakewell. Front row: Rickinson (below Hussey). Blackborow lay incapacitated in his bag.

wrote. He was in considerably higher spirits since moving into the hut, and once again responsive to the stern beauty of the changing light upon the glacier faces and cliffs.

"A sunrise of bright red clouds reflected in the mirrory stillness of the bay I am utterly powerless to describe," he wrote. "The vast ice facade presented to the sea, assumed a bright pea green hue with isolated areas of emerald! . . . Violet tints & purples lingered on the snow slopes. . . . The rocky scarps ordinarily a greyblack, still kept their natural color but appeared to shine with a golden veneer."

"Oh if I only had my cameras," he wrote elsewhere, referring to his lost professional gear. All his surviving glass plates and cinematographic film, stored in their hermetically sealed cannisters, had been cached in a snow hole, along with the ship's log, the expedition's scientific records, and his photograph album.

Winter had set in. May is the southern hemisphere's equivalent of November, and by midmonth the gravel beach was hidden beneath a layer of ice, and an ice foot extended on both sides of the spit. Everything was covered with snow. The temperatures on Elephant Island, situated above the Antarctic Circle, were not so severe as those the men had encountered on the floes—11° Fahrenheit was considered low— but because they were constantly wet and exposed to gales approaching 80 miles an hour, they often felt colder.

The men were by no means starving, but they were always hungry, and the unrelenting monotony of the virtually carnivorous diet was wearing on their minds as well as their bodies. From time to time, Wild doled out rations of special treats remaining from the eclectic stores they still carried with them. The last of a pearl barley pudding with jam, for example, made a great impression on the company. Lees was horrified at this extravagance, and recorded that it should have been spread over several days, instead of being devoured at one sitting. But Hurley's reaction justifies this indulgence:

"Fine Barley pudding for lunch," he wrote. "The remnants also of jam. The meal gave us great pleasure, inasmuch as we have not had a full cereal meal for two & ½ months." The almost forgotten sensation of being satisfied at the end of a meal, together with the sense of an "occasion," appears to have done wonders for morale, and in a sense made the meal go farther.

The days grew shorter, with sunlight only from nine in the morning until three in the afternoon. Wild's "Lash up and stow" now served only as a wake-up call, for with the men spending up to seventeen hours a day in their bags, there was no need to stow them. The longer darkness made it harder to read, and the few available diversions were circumscribed yet more.

"Everyone spent the day rotting in their bags with blubber and tobacco smoke,"

Elephant Island
"I make this entry on the highest point of our Camping Spit. . . . The weather is delightful: bright warm sunshine & dead calm. Cape Wild is a narrow neck of land jutting out from the mainland some 220 to 250 yards. . . . The ocean termination is a precipitous rocky bluff ranging to about 20 feet in height which is guarded oceanwise by a rocky islet that presents a flat jagged face 300 feet in height, called the Gnomon. . . . I secure photographs. (Hurley, diary)

Greenstreet wrote bluntly. "So passes another goddam rotten day." In addition to various nautical books and copies of Walter Scott and Browning, five volumes of the *Encyclopaedia Britannica* had been saved from the *Endurance* library. The most entertainment per page was afforded by Marston's *Penny Cookbook*, which inspired many imaginary meals.

Bartering with food became the principle pastime. Lees in particular was a demon for this, his propensity for saving odds and ends and his access to the stores ensuring that he always had a small stock of goods with which to negotiate.

"McLeod exchanged a cake of nut-food with Blackborrow for seven half penguin steaks payable at the rate of half a steak daily at breakfast time," wrote Lees. "Wild exchanged his penguin steak last night for one biscuit with Stephenson. The other day the latter asked me if I would give him a cake of nut-food for all his lump sugar due i.e. at the rate of six lumps per week, and Holness did likewise."

As the hours of darkness increased, the singsongs to the accompaniment of Hussey's banjo played a more important role. While the wind raged outside, the men lay in their bags, still dressed in their perpetually wet clothing, and sang heartily all the familiar songs that evoked cozy, secure times gone by aboard the *Endurance*. Sea chanties—"Captain Stormalong," "A Sailor's Alphabet"—were always favorites, especially when rendered in Wild's fine bass, or by Marston, who had the best voice of anyone in the company. Inventing new songs, or improvising new words to familiar tunes, a genre at which Hussey was a master, allowed the men to let off steam by taking jabs at one another without causing offense:

When faces turn pale 'neath the soot and the grime,
When eyes start in terror as if caught in some crime,
When we beg on our knees to be let off this time,
Then you know that Kerr's threatened to sing.

The overall health of the party was not as good as it had been at Patience Camp. As Lees noted, any of the men would have preferred the dry cold of the floes to the humid cold of Elephant Island. A number of cases of septic wounds and other minor complaints were registered, and Rickinson, while more or less recovered from his heart ailment, was suffering from saltwater boils that would not heal. Hudson was still "done up" and had developed a huge, painful abscess on his left buttock. Greenstreet was also suffering from frostbite, although not as seriously as Blackborow.

Blackborow's condition had become so grave that Macklin and McIlroy, who were closely monitoring him, had braced themselves for the possibility of having to amputate his feet. By June, his right foot seemed to be on the mend, but the toes of the left foot had become gangrenous and needed to be removed. Requiring a temperature high enough to vaporize their scant supply of chloroform, they waited for the first mild day to perform the operation.

On June 15, all hands except for Wild, Hurley, How, and other invalids were sent outside while the Snuggery was converted into an operating theater. A platform of food boxes covered with blankets served as an operating table, and Hurley stoked the bogie stove with penguin skins, eventually raising the temperature to 79°. The few surgical instruments were boiled in the hoosh pot. Macklin and McIlroy stripped to their undershirts, the cleanest layer of clothing they possessed. While Macklin administered the anaesthetic, McIlroy performed the surgery. Hudson averted his face; Hurley, characteristically unsqueamish, found it fascinating, as did Greenstreet, who was lying nearby recovering from rheumatism.

"Blackborow had an operation on his toes today," wrote Greenstreet, who was suffering from frostbite and rheumatism, "having all the toes of his left foot taken off about ¼″ stumps being left. I was one of the few who watched the operation and it was most interesting. The poor beggar behaved splendidly."

Wild, who lent a hand in the operation, showed no revulsion as McIlroy slit and peeled back the skin of Blackborow's foot.

"He is a hard case," Macklin wrote.

When the operation was completed, the rest of the party were called in again, while Blackborow slept off the chloroform. He was a great favorite of all hands, and his cheerfulness both before and after the ordeal was much admired. Lees was impressed by his fortitude too, but the operation had caused him personal concern.

"Practically the whole of the available anaesthetic was used up," he wrote, "so that if I have to have my leg off, not that there is anything whatever the matter with it at present. . . . I shall have to have it done without anaesthetic."

His consternation inspired Hussey to write new verses:

> *When the Doctors dance round with joy on their faces,*
> *And sharpen up knives and take saws from their cases,*
> *When Mack spits on his hands and Mick hoists up his braces,*
> *Then you know that the Colonel's gone sick.*

The addition of several small windowpanes, made of a chronometer case and piece of celluloid that Hurley had stashed in the pages of a book, cast murky new light inside the hut, reawakening the men to the general squalor of the conditions in which they lived. Grease, blubber smoke and soot, reindeer hairs, seal and penguin blood, melting guano were embedded into every crack and fiber of the hut and their few possessions. Scraps of meat dropped in the darkness festered unseen on the floor. At night a two-gallon petrol can was used as a urinal, so as to spare the men a long, stumbling journey past a row of sleeping bags, out into the icy night. Wild's rule was that the man who filled the can to within two inches of capacity was responsible for taking it outside and emptying it; but all hands became adept at gauging the volume remaining in the can by the noise it made as it got filled. If it sounded as if the two-inch limit was nearly reached, a man would wait in his bag for someone whose need was more urgent to precede him.

Midwinter Day, June 22, was celebrated as it had been on *Endurance* with a feast, songs, and facetious sketches, all performed by the men from their sleeping bags. Like Shackleton, Wild took care to punctuate the monotonous existence with any excuse for an "occasion." Toasts were drunk to the King, the Returning Sun, and the Boss and Crew of the *Caird* with a new concoction consisting of Clark's 90 percent methylated spirit (a preservative for specimens), sugar, water, and ginger (a tin of which, thought to contain pepper, had been brought along by mistake). This "Gut Rot 1916" became greatly popular, especially with Wild himself. The toast to "Sweethearts and Wives" was still drunk on Saturdays.

July brought warmer, wetter weather. The great glacier at the head of the inlet was dropping enormous chunks of ice, which cracked off with the noise of a rifle shot and sent up huge waves upon impact with the water below. A more serious problem, however, was the accumulation of melted snow and ice—and penguin guano—on the hut floor.

"Thaw water having risen to the uncomfortable extent of rendering the shingly floor a sludgy mess, we set about the smelly occupation of bailing out and reshin-

Ice Stalactites

"July 5, 1916: Pleasant calm day though dull. During the morning go walking with Wild. We visit a neighboring cavern in the glacier which was adorned with a magnificence of icicles. Fine shawlike stalactites covered the walls & the roof was adorned with a finish of curiously carved and footlike stalactites." (Hurley, diary)

gling," wrote Hurley. "By means of a "sumphole" some 80 gallons of cesspit odorous liquid was removed." This unpleasant process was to be repeated throughout the month.

Adding to the general edginess was the fact that the tobacco supply of all but the most frugal and self-disciplined had given out.

"Holness, one of the sailors, sits up in the cold every night after everyone else has turned in gazing intently at Wild & McIlroy in the hopes that one of them will give him the unsmokeable part of a toilet-paper cigarette," wrote Lees. This crisis elicited a hitherto undetected inventiveness amongst the sailors. With the dedication of laboratory scientists, they methodically tested every combustible fiber as a possible tobacco substitute. Great hopes were pinned on a scheme devised by Bakewell, who collected the pipes of the entire company and boiled them in the hoosh pot together with sennegrass, which was used to insulate their finnesko boots; his theory was that residual nicotine would imbue the grass with its flavor.

"A strong aroma as of a prairie fire pervades the atmosphere," wrote Hurley. The experiment was a failure, but Bakewell at least was philosophical. "Had we had plenty to eat and to smoke, our minds would have been on our real peril," he wrote, "which would have been very dangerous to the morale of the camp."

Smoking was not the only pleasure of which the crew were deprived. Wild had put a halt to the food bartering after Lees managed to garner many weeks' supplies of sugar from the improvident sailors; invoking the opinion of the doctors, Wild informed Lees that the carbohydrate element he had so assiduously procured was necessary for the welfare of the men. Toasts with methylated spirits had become markedly more frequent in July, but this supply too was dwindling, as were, more importantly, the biscuit and precious Nutfood. The powdered milk was gone. Soon there would be only penguin or seal to look forward to for every meal. But the monotony and unhealthfulness of the diet were not all that were becoming wearisome; also taking a toll was the unending need for slaughter.

"About 30 Gentoo Penguins came ashore & I am pleased the weather was too bad to slay them," wrote Hurley. "We are heartily sick of being compelled to kill every bird that comes ashore for food."

August 13 was so bright and so mild that a general spring cleaning was undertaken and sleeping bags and groundcloths were spread out to dry. Blackborow was carried out to enjoy the sun; he had spent every day of the four months they had been on Elephant Island inside his bag, without complaint. The fine weather continued, and several of the men collected limpets and seaweed from low tidal pools; boiled in seawater, they provided a welcome novelty to their diet.

The weather continued to fluctuate erratically, with more fine brilliant days followed by a northeast blizzard that dumped heavy snow, forming drifts up to four feet high around the hut. On August 19, the pack was so dense that no water at all was visible from the lookout bluff. The expectant atmosphere with which the month had opened now gave way to a mood of increasing anxiety; August had always been the very latest month speculated for a possible rescue.

"All are becoming anxious for the safety of the *Caird* as allowing a fair margin of time for contingencies, [a ship] should have made her appearance by now," wrote Hurley. "The weather is wretched. A stagnant calm of air & ocean alike, the latter obscured by heavy pack & a dense wet mist hangs like a pall over land & sea. The silence is extremely oppressive."

Now for the first time the possibility of Shackleton's not returning was openly discussed; more ominously, Wild had quietly issued an order that all cordwood and nails were to be hoarded—in the event that a boat journey had to be made to Deception Island.

Muggy, wet weather plagued them on the 21st, melting eight inches of new snow which seeped under the boats. Though the men had known that Blackborow's foot was not healing properly, it now became generally known that the swelling and inflammation indicated osteomyelitis, or infection of the bone.

The weather continued to be warm, and on the 24th, Marston was discovered sunbathing. On the 25th it turned dull and damp, and on the 26th it began to rain again. For all these days, not a breath of wind seemed to stir the ice or water. On the 27th, Wild, anticipating a thaw, set the men digging snow drift away from the hut. The work continued on the 28th, and although it was arduous, most enjoyed the unaccustomed exercise.

August 29 was clear, with a strong wind. "[P]reparations are being pushed along for sending one of our two boats," wrote Lees. "Wild has it all nicely cut & dried, & has revealed his plans to the favoured few. He and four other members are to go in the *Dudley Docker*, and will make their way carefully along under the lee of the land from island to island of the South Shetlands . . . until they reach Deception Island about 250 miles away to our S.W." According to this plan, the *Docker* would set out about October 5, in order to catch the whalers who plied the waters around Deception Island.

Simple enough in theory, the plan represented a course of action no one wished to take. The mere thought of another boat journey was daunting enough in the best of circumstances. As it was, the most valuable equipment had left with the *Caird*, and there now remained only a jib, old tent cloths in lieu of a mainsail, and five oars; even the mast of the *Dudley Docker* had been used to strengthen the keel of the *Caird*. Above all, the departure of the *Dudley Docker* from Elephant Island would be an acknowledgment that somewhere in the broad southern ocean the *Caird* and all hands had been lost.

August 30 dawned clear and cold. All hands worked at removing snow drift, but stopped at 11 a.m. to take advantage of the low tide and calm sea to catch limpets for the evening meal. At 12:45, most of the men turned in for "hoosh oh," a lunch of boiled seal's backbone, while Marston and Hurley remained outside, shelling limpets.

Wild was just serving the meal when the sound of Marston's running steps was heard outside—undoubtedly he was late for lunch. Moments later, he stuck his head into the hut, panting.

"Wild, there's a ship," he said, excitedly. "Shall we light a fire?"

"Before there was time for a reply there was a rush of members tumbling over one another," Lees reported, "all mixed up with mugs of seal hoosh making a simultaneous dive for the door-hole which was immediately torn to shreds."

Outside, Hurley, ever resourceful, ignited paraffin, blubber, and sennegrass, creating an explosive blaze, but little smoke. It did not matter; the ship was headed for Cape Wild.

"There she lay," wrote Lees, "barely a mile off, a very little black ship, apparently a steam tug, not at all the wooden polar ice-breaking craft we expected to see." While they gazed in wonder, Macklin ran to the "flagpole" and hoisted his Burberry jacket as high as the running gear permitted, which was about half-mast. Meanwhile, Hudson and Lees carried Blackborow outside, and arrived in time to see the mystery ship raise, to their bewilderment, the Chilean naval ensign.

Cheering loudly, the men watched in excitement as the ship drew closer. Anchoring within 500 feet of the shore, the small tug lowered a boat; and in her the men recognized the sturdy, square-set figure of Shackleton, and then Crean.

"I felt jolly near blubbing for a bit & could not speak for several minutes," wrote Wild.

"Then there was some real live cheers given," recalled Bakewell. Breathlessly, the men waited as Shackleton approached. When he was in hearing distance they called out in unison, "All well!"

Worsley had been with Shackleton on the deck of the *Yelcho* when they first spotted the island. Their hearts had sunk when they saw a flag at half-mast, but gazing with painful intensity through his binoculars, Shackleton had made out the twenty-two figures on shore.

"He put his glasses back in their case and turned to me, his face showing more emotion than I had ever known it show before," wrote Worsley. "Crean had joined us, and we were all unable to speak. . . . It sounds trite, but years literally seemed to drop from him as he stood before us."

In one hour, the entire company of Elephant Island and their few possessions were

Rescuing the crew from Elephant Island

"30 August — Wednesday — Day of Wonders." (Hurley, diary)

aboard the *Yelcho*, Hurley bringing along his cannisters of plates and film, and Greenstreet the log of the *Endurance*. Shackleton, ever mindful of the treacherous ice, resisted invitations to come ashore to examine the Snuggery; he was eager to be out beyond the pack line as quickly as possible.

Lees was the last to leave; he had been standing by the hut in readiness to give the Boss a tour of the premises. Only after the last boat trip had been made did he appear on the beach, frantically waving his arms, and practically diving into the boat when it put around.

From the bridge of the *Yelcho*, Worsley intently watched the rescue.

"2.10 All Well!" he recorded in his log. "At last! 2.15 full speed ahead."

The adventure was over; and almost immediately it seemed as if things had not really been so bad. Somehow, in the day-to-day running of the camp, Wild had managed to make their predicament seem merely uncomfortable rather than desperate.

"I am not very susceptible to emotions . . . ," Hurley wrote. "Yet as those noble peaks faded away in the mist, I could scarce repress feelings of sadness to leave forever the land that has rained on us its bounty and been salvation. Our hut, a lone relic of our habitation, will become a centre around which coveys of penguins will assemble to gaze with curiosity & deliberate its origin. Good old Elephant Isle."

Shackleton had much to tell both his men and the outside world. But the letter he dashed off to his wife on landing again in Punta Arenas stated only the essentials.

"I have done it. Damn the Admiralty. . . . Not a life lost and we have been through Hell."

The Yelcho, *triumphant. This photograph capturing the little tug's return to port was taken by a Mr. Vega, who was, according to Hurley, the town's leading photographer.*

"3rd September Sunday. Beautiful sunrise, with fine mist effects over the hills & distant mts. surrounding Punta Arenas. Shortly after 7 a.m. Sir E. rowed ashore & telephoned our arrival on to Punta Arenas, so that the populace might roll up and greet us after church, we being due to arrive at 12 noon. The Yelcho *was bedecked with flags. . . . On nearing the jetty we were deafened by the tooting of whistles & cheering motor craft, which was taken up by the vast gathering on the piers & water-fronts." (Hurley, diary)*

"To My Comrades"

So on the deep and open sea I set
Forth, with a single ship and that small band
Of comrades that had never left me yet.

— DANTE, "VOYAGE OF ULYSSES," *L'Inferno*

"Tell me, when was the war over?" Shackleton had asked Sørlle, on arriving at Stromness Station after crossing South Georgia.

"The war is not over," Sørlle had replied. "Millions are being killed. Europe is mad. The world is mad."

During their ordeal on the ice, the war had been a frequent topic of conversation, with the men chiefly concerned that they would miss it entirely by the time they got home. Before boarding the *Yelcho*, Shackleton had taken pains to collect mail that had been waiting for the men at South Georgia, as well as newspapers, to give them some idea of what they had missed in the nearly two years they had been out of touch with the world.

"'Opinions have changed on all sorts of subjects,'" Lees reports Shackleton as telling them on the *Yelcho*. "'They call it the Roll of Honour now instead of the Casualty List.'"

"The reader may not realize quite how difficult it was for us to envisage nearly two years of the most stupendous war of history," wrote Shackleton, in his own book, *South*. "The locking of the armies in the trenches, the sinking of the *Lusitania*, the murder of Nurse Cavell, the use of poison-gas and liquid fire, the submarine warfare, the Gallipoli campaign, the hundred other incidents of the war, almost stunned us at first. . . . I suppose our experience was unique. No other civilized men could have been as blankly ignorant of world-shaking happenings as we were when we reached Stromness Whaling Station."

The war had changed everything—and most of all the heroic ideal. With millions of Europe's young men dead, Britain was not particularly interested in survival stories. The news of the *Endurance* expedition was so extraordinary that it could not fail to fill popular headlines; but Shackleton's official reception was markedly cool. Facetiously describing his arrival in Stanley, in the Falklands, after the failure of the *Southern Sky* rescue mission, the paper *John Bull* gave this account.

"Not a soul in Stanley seemed to care one scrap [about his arrival]! Not a single flag was flown. . . . An old kelper remarked, "'E ought ter 'ave been at the war long ago instead of messing about on icebergs.'"

In Punta Arenas, Shackleton and his men received an almost riotous welcome, with the town's various nationalities—including the Germans, with whom Britain was at war—pouring out with bands and flags to greet them. Shackleton had cannily stopped off in Río Seco, some six miles away, to alert Punta Arenas by telephone of his imminent arrival. The Foreign Office was quick to see publicity value in his popularity, and encouraged Shackleton to call upon those governments that had come to his assistance. And so with a handful of his men, he went to Santiago, Buenos Aires, and Montevideo. Pointedly, he paid no visit to the British Falklands.

The *Endurance* expedition ended on October 8, 1916, in Buenos Aires, but Shackleton still had work to do. The other half of the Imperial Trans-Antarctic Expedition, the Ross Sea depot-laying party on the opposite side of the globe, had gone adrift, literally: The expedition's ship *Aurora* had come untethered from her mooring and then been prevented from returning to "port" by the pack ice. Another saga of survival—involving one of the most formidable feats of man-hauling sledging in Antarctic exploration—had unfolded on the snow and ice where Shackleton had first won renown as a polar explorer. Three lives had been lost. Shackleton was therefore bound back to the Antarctic to pick up the pieces of his expedition.

At the Buenos Aires railway station, Shackleton said goodbye to his men who had come to see him off. It was the last time so many members of the expedition—all but Blackborow and Hudson—would be gathered together.

"We have properly broken up," Macklin wrote. With few exceptions, most were to be on their way back to Britain. Blackborow was in the hospital in Punta Arenas and was the object of doting attention from the city's female population; Bakewell was staying on.

"When I joined the expedition, I asked that I might be paid off at Buenos Aires on our return," wrote Bakewell. "Sir Ernest consented to my wish and now I was at the parting of the way. I had to say good-bye to the finest group of men that it has ever been my good fortune to be with."

Hudson—the invalid, the indisposed, he of the "general breakdown"—had already left, eager to take up his commission and be of service to his country. While on Elephant Island, the two doctors had drained his terrible abscess, which had grown to the size of a football, and this operation seemed to have put him on his way to recovery. The detached stupor in which he had reportedly spent most of the time on Elephant Island may have resulted from the fever that would have inevitably accompanied such a deep infection.

Hurley, having quickly tired of the celebratory receptions, spent long days in a darkroom made available to him by a generous local photographer.

"All the plates which were exposed on the wreck nearly twelve months ago turned out excellently," he wrote. "The small Kodak film suffered through the protracted keeping but will be printable."

From Punta Arenas, Shackleton telegraphed long articles to the *Daily Chronicle* in London.

"Relief of the Marooned Explorers." "Shackleton Safe." "Shackleton's Men Rescued." The stories continued to run well into December.

Hurley arrived in Liverpool on November 11.

"The customs occupied considerable time," he wrote, "especially with the film, which was weighed—a method of estimating the length & charged an import duty of 5d per foot. The entire film netted a customs revenue of 120 pounds." Travelling to London by train, he went straight to the offices of the *Daily Chronicle* and handed over the film to Ernest Perris. For the next three months, Hurley worked single-mindedly on the development of his photographs, his motion picture film, lantern slides to be used in lectures, and the preparation of albums of selected images. Dramatic spreads appeared in some of the papers (the *Chronicle*, the *Daily Mail*, the *Sphere*), and he was greatly satisfied with a display of his Paget Colour Plates at the Polytechnic Hall; here, projected on a screen eighteen feet square, the *Endurance* soared out of the darkness under a luminous yet icy sky, once more to grapple with her fate.

As early as November 15, Hurley had decided to return to South Georgia to acquire wildlife photographs, hoping to reproduce the ones he had been forced to jettison on the ice. The sojourn in England was pleasant, despite the fact that "London possesses the worst climate I have ever yet experienced, as regards producing colds and sickness." During this period, he frequently saw James, Wordie, Clark, and Greenstreet.

The South Georgia trip was successful, and after several weeks of characteristically intense work, Hurley returned to London in June 1917, and handed over another batch of film and plates to Perris. The film, *In the Grip of the Polar Pack*, was released in 1919, after the war, to much acclaim.

Why Shackleton had never liked and indeed deeply mistrusted Hurley is not clear; he had taken considerable pains to cater to his vanity on the ice, including him in all important counsels. For his part, Hurley expressed his admiration for Shackleton both openly and privately in his diary. Hurley was bombastic, vain, arrogant, high-handed, not easy to get on with—but above all he was eminently capable. Stoves, electrical plants, improvised boat pumps, stone galley walls—many contrivances that had materially benefitted the party throughout the expedition—had been the work of his huge hands. Was this the problem? Did this multitalented, hard as nails, cocksure Aussie strike Shackleton as being the kind of man who might in certain situations have felt himself to be above Shackleton's own authority?

The film went a long way in paying off the expeditionary debts awaiting Shackleton when he at last returned to England in May 1917. After the relief of the Ross Sea party, he made a whirlwind lecture tour across America, which had just entered the war. Now, his immediate concern was to secure some position in the war effort. Although legally exempt from service at age forty-two, and bone-weary, Shackleton knew that service of some kind would be essential to winning support for whatever venture he might undertake in the future. His return to England had received scant attention; there would be no more heroes who were not war heroes.

Months passed. Thirty of his men from both the Weddell and Ross Sea parties were actively in service, and still Shackleton could find no commission. He was drinking and restless, spending little time at home; in London, he could often be found in the company of his American mistress, Rosalind Chetwynd. Eventually, through the intervention of Sir Edward Carson, former First Lord of the Admiralty (and former legal defense for the Marquis of Queensberry in the libel suit brought against him by Oscar Wilde), Shackleton was sent on a propaganda mission to South America. His vague assignment was to raise morale, promote the British war effort, and report on the propaganda efforts already in place.

He left for Buenos Aires in October 1917, and was back in London in April 1918. He had still not had the satisfaction of being in uniform. Once again, he embarked on rounds of dead-end interviews, attempting to obtain a proper commission. A series of various small commissions eventually landed him in Spitsbergen and finally in Murmansk, Russia, where his official title was "staff officer in charge of Arctic Transport." At least he was with some old companions. At his request, Frank Wild had been released from duties in Archangel to be his assistant. McIlroy, who had been gravely wounded in Ypres, had been invalided out of the army. Hussey was there and later Macklin, who had been in France. Also sent to this polar outpost were a few of Scott's old men, who remained unsympathetic, if not hostile, to Shackleton. That Scott and his men had died of scurvy was still officially denied, as it implied misman-agement; the men of the *Endurance* had been in the ice for nearly two years without a sign of this disease, thanks to Shackleton's insistence, from the first days of the *Endurance*'s entrapment in the ice, on the consumption of fresh meat.

When the war ended, Shackleton was adrift again. While still in New Zealand, he had dictated the most critical parts of *South* to Edward Saunders, the collaborator on his first book. In 1919, *South* was at last published, written by Saunders and drawing from Shackleton's extensive dictation and the diaries of the expedition members. Given this method of composition, the account is remarkably accurate. Names and dates are sometimes muddled and so, occasionally, is the order of events (such as on the *James Caird* journey). It downplays a number of episodes but omits surprisingly few. There is no mention of McNish's rebellion, for example. Shackleton dedicated the book "To My Comrades."

The book was critically acclaimed and sold well. Shackleton, however, received no royalties from it. The executors of one of his expedition's benefactors, Sir Robert Lucas-Tooth, who had died in 1915, hounded him for repayment. By way of settlement, Shackleton handed over all rights to *South*, his only asset.

At the end of the war, Shackleton was characteristically broke, in not particularly good health and at loose ends. He was now rarely with his wife, for whom he nonetheless continued to express devotion, and lived mainly in the Mayfair flat of his mistress. Against his every inclination, financial necessity compelled him to hit the lecture circuit, telling the story of the thwarted *Endurance* expedition, now years past, to half-filled halls, while behind him, Hurley's luminous lantern slides evoked haunting memories. In preparing these slides, Hurley had perfected an ingenious method of composite image making, whereby photographs of wildlife were superimposed upon stretches of empty ice, for example, or any number of scenes were set against spectacularly back-lit clouds—his trademark. The purpose of the photographs had always been commercial, and Hurley seems to have had no compunction about this kind of manipulation.

In 1920, Shackleton suddenly announced a yearning to return to polar regions—whether north or south did not seem to matter. One last time, he hustled his way around London, seeking sponsorship, until eventually an old school chum from Dulwich, John Quiller Rowett, came to his aid, agreeing to underwrite the entire ill-defined enterprise.

Animated as he had not been in years, Shackleton sent word to old *Endurance* hands that he was headed south once again. McIlroy and Wild came from Nyasaland, in southern Africa, where they had been farming cotton; Green returned as cook.

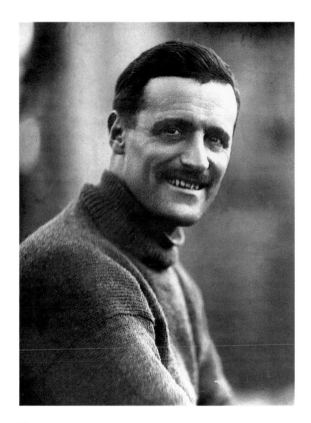

J. A. McIlroy

Worldly and debonair, McIlroy had travelled widely in the East before joining the Endurance *as ship's surgeon.*

Hussey came with his banjo, as well as Macklin, who had become one of Shackleton's closest friends. McLeod, the old shellback from *Nimrod* days, returned, as well as Kerr; Worsley was to be skipper.

Their ship, the *Quest*, was a lumbering former sealer that required repairs in every port of call. No sledging dogs were on board this time, just a single canine pet, named Query. Even as she set out, it was unclear exactly where the *Quest* was headed or what the purpose of this "expedition" was; plans ranged from circumnavigating the Antarctic continent to looking for Captain Kidd's treasure. It didn't matter. All on board were there to bask in the atmosphere of adventure, or of memories.

The *Quest* departed from London on September 17, 1921, seen off by a large, cheering crowd. Film footage from the expedition shows Shackleton as a somewhat stout, middle-aged man wearing suspenders: One could picture him with rolled-up trousers dabbling in the shallows at the beach. All his companions sensed he was not his former self, and Macklin and McIlroy were gravely concerned about his health. In Rio, Shackleton suffered a heart attack but refused to be examined, let alone turn back. He recovered, and the *Quest* continued south.

En route, the *Quest* encountered an unexpected apparition—an old-time five-masted square-rigged ship, the *France*. Excitedly, Shackleton's men ran their ship close by in order to take photographs. It was, for these veterans of the heroic age, a brush with an all-but-vanished era, and they regarded the vessel wistfully from their own lumbering ship.

On January 4, after a stormy passage, the *Quest* arrived in South Georgia.

"At last," wrote Shackleton in his diary, "we came to anchor in Grytviken. How familiar the coast seemed as we passed down: we saw with full interest the places we struggled over after the boat journey. . . . The old familiar smell of dead whale permeates everything. It is a strange and curious place. . . . A wonderful evening.

In the darkening twilight I saw a lone star hover
Gem-like above the bay."

"The Boss says . . . quite frankly that he does not know what he will do after S. Georgia," Macklin had written, only five days earlier.

In South Georgia Shackleton found a number of the old-stagers still manning the station. He was warmly greeted by Fridthjof Jacobsen, still Grytviken's manager, and the men went ashore and looked over the old haunts where they had passed a month while the *Endurance* lay at anchor. Enjoying the beautiful weather, they went walking in the hills, then sat and watched the gulls and terns. In the spot where they had exercised the sledging dogs, they now threw sticks for Query.

At the end of the day, they returned to the ship and had dinner on board. After the meal, Shackleton rose and jokingly announced, "To-morrow we'll keep Christmas." At two in the morning, Macklin was summoned by a whistle to Shackleton's cabin.

"I noticed that although it was a cold night he had only one blanket, and asked him if he had no others," wrote Macklin in a revealing passage, which suggests that he had for some time acted as a kind of furtive nurse to the Boss. "He replied that they were in his bottom drawer and he could not be bothered getting them out. I started to do so, but he said, 'Never mind to-night, I can stand the cold.' However, I went back to my cabin and got a heavy Jaeger blanket from my bunk, which I tucked around him."

Macklin sat with him quietly for some minutes, and took the opportunity to suggest that he might take things easy in the future.

"You are always wanting me to give up something," replied the Boss. "What do you want me to give up now?" These were Shackleton's last words. A massive heart attack took him suddenly, and he died at 2:50 a.m.; he was only forty-seven years old. Macklin, upon whom fell the task of conducting an autopsy, diagnosed the cause of death as "atheroma of the coronary arteries," a long-standing condition exacerbated, in Macklin's opinion, by "overstrain during a period of debility." Macklin had in mind not the more recent ordeal of the *Endurance* expedition, but the strain of his Farthest South, as far back as 1909.

Hussey volunteered to accompany Shackleton's body back to England, but in Montevideo, he was intercepted by a message from Shackleton's wife, Emily, requesting that her husband be buried in South Georgia; the thought of his restless spirit closeted in the narrow rank and file of a British cemetery was insupportable. Hussey turned back, and on March 5, Shackleton was laid to rest among the Norwegian whalers who had, perhaps, above all other men on earth best comprehended his achievements. The small band of men who had stuck with him to the end were at his simple funeral. Hussey played Brahms's "Lullaby" on his banjo, then Shackleton's spirit was left alone with the harsh grandeur of the landscape that had forged his greatness.

Although Shackleton had dreamt his whole life of achieving success in ordinary, civilian circumstances, he seemed to understand that he would never do so.

"Sometimes I think I am no good at anything but being away in the wilds just with men," Shackleton had written to his wife in 1919. He would be remembered not so much for his own accomplishment—the 1909 expedition that attained the farthest South—as for what he was capable of drawing out of others.

"Shackleton's popularity among those he led was due to the fact that he was not the sort of man who could do only big and spectacular things," Worsley wrote.

"When occasion demanded he would attend personally to the smallest details. . . . Sometimes it would appear to the thoughtless that his care amounted almost to fussiness, and it was only afterwards that we understood the supreme importance of his ceaseless watchfulness." Behind every calculated word and gesture lay the single-minded determination to do what was best for his men. At the core of Shackleton's gift for leadership in crisis was an adamantine conviction that quite ordinary individuals were capable of heroic feats if the circumstances required; the weak and the strong could and *must* survive together. The mystique that Shackleton acquired as a leader may partly be attributed to the fact that he elicited from his men strength and endurance they had never imagined they possessed; he ennobled them.

Shackleton did not attain the recognition accorded to Scott. England had room for only one great polar explorer in its pantheon, and coming after the First World War, the memory of the doomed, tragic youthful hero who had died in bringing honor to his country was better suited to the national mood of mourning.

Shackleton nonetheless achieved an unexpected place in the collective imagination. His account of the mysterious presence that had guided him, Worsley, and Crean across South Georgia haunted T. S. Eliot, who evoked it in *The Waste Land:*

> *Who is the third who walks always beside you?*
> *When I count, there are only you and I together*
> *But when I look ahead up the white road*
> *There is always another one walking beside you.*

The *James Caird*, the most tangible relic of his endeavors, eventually made her way to Shackleton's old school, Dulwich College, where she still resides.

After Shackleton's death, the *Quest* doggedly continued under the command of Frank Wild. At the end of this somewhat meandering journey, Wild took the ship to within sight of Elephant Island, although he did not land.

"Few of us thought when we left it last that it would ever be our fate to see it again," Macklin wrote. "Ah what memories what memories!—they rush to one like a great flood & bring tears to ones eyes, & as I sit & try to write a great rush of feeling comes over me & I find I cannot express myself or what I feel. Once more I see the little boat, Frankie Wild's hut, dark & dirty, but a snug little shelter all the same. Once more I see the old faces & hear the old voices—old friends scattered everywhere. But to express all I feel is impossible."

Although the world to which Shackleton and his men returned was indeed greatly changed from the one they had left behind, it must be allowed that the "old age," and its skills and values, were in decline even as the *Endurance* departed from London in 1914. When Shackleton had been in Buenos Aires, looking for replacements for his crew, he had been especially pleased to find Bakewell, whose years of experience in sailing vessels was becoming an increasingly rare commodity in an age when steam travel was slowly claiming the seas. Shackleton's entrepreneurial method of financing his expedition was itself indicative of a new order, one in which energetic, ambitious men would seek to force their own opportunity, with or without the kind of patronage that had blessed Scott. The *Endurance* had never been intended for heroic endeavor, but was originally built as a tourist vessel to convey wealthy clients on polar safaris to the Arctic; this was why she had been such a comfortable, well-equipped little vessel. Likewise, in this increasingly sophisticated age, photo and story rights for whatever adventure might transpire had been sold well in advance; that a book would be the outcome of their experience was never completely out of the crew's mind, and at critical junctures Shackleton had made sure that the diarists and Hurley preserved their work.

"With a boat . . . we could reach the seals we occasionally see out on the floes," Lees had written, in June 1916, while they were on Elephant Island. "But if we had everything we wanted we should have no privations to write about and that would be a serious loss to the 'book.' Privations make a book sell like anything."

Many of the *Endurance* crew did very well in their post-expedition life, but others did not adjust to the loss of the old order that had been swept away by the war. The lives of the men who had participated in one of the greatest survival stories in expeditionary history took very different courses.

In February 1918, the London *Telegraph* ran a half-column story under the heading "Antarctic Expedition: The Polar Medal." There followed a list of the Imperial Trans-Antarctic Expedition members and a brief account of their ordeal. One of the awards was already posthumous; four months after landing the *James Caird* on South Georgia Island—three weeks after arriving in England—Tim McCarthy was killed at his gun in the Channel. Not much later, Alf Cheetham, who was said to have crossed the Antarctic Circle more times than any of the other men, would be drowned when his minesweeper was torpedoed by a German submarine off the River Humber, a few weeks before Armistice.

Strikingly, four names are missing from the roster: Shackleton had not recommended Stephenson and Holness for the medal, nor two members of the *James Caird* crew, Vincent and McNish. Vincent's collapse and McNish's brief rebellion had cost them dearly. Because there was never a formal award ceremony, the majority of the expedition members did not learn for many years that some of their companions had been excluded.

Macklin, who had come to be very close to Shackleton, was shaken when he did learn. He wrote to one of Shackleton's biographers:

Of all men in the party no-one more deserved recognition than the old carpenter. . . . He was not only a skilled carpenter but a very knowledgeable seaman. All the work he did was first class . . . and his efforts to save the crushed *Endurance*, standing most of the time in icy water, deserved all praise. . . . Chippy had an unfortunate manner . . . and he did not hesitate to give back-chat to anyone with whom he did not agree, including Shackleton, who I do not think minded very much, and particularly to Worsley for whose erratic temperament and wild actions he had no admiration at all, and did not hesitate to let him know. Worsley as a result disliked Chippy—it was mutual antipathy which led to the incident on the floe. I think Worsley may have influenced Shackleton in this respect in the later stages of the expedition when they were so much together. I would regard the withholding of the Polar Medal from McNeish as a grave injustice. I think too that the withholding of the medal from the three trawlermen was a bit hard. They were perhaps not very endearing characters but they never let the expedition down.

After coming home to England, McNish returned to sea. Throughout his diary, he had addressed affectionate asides to his "Loved One" and daughter; but this unknown woman from Cathcart, Scotland, does not seem to have remained in his life. He retired and lived with his son and his family for some years before one day announcing that he was going to New Zealand.

"And what are you thinking of, a man of your age?" his daughter-in-law remonstrated. "Don't worry, lass, I've got a job there," said Chippy. A few days later, a horse-drawn cart arrived to take his old sea chest, and that was the last his family saw or heard of him.

McNish complained that his bones ached permanently after the *James Caird* journey. Ill health and drink left him unable to work, and eventually he became destitute. To the seamen of the Wellington docks, however, the carpenter of the *James Caird* was a hero, and the watchman turned a blind eye whenever the old man crawled into a wharf shed at night to sleep under a tarpaulin. A monthly collection was taken up by the wharf brotherhood for him and others down on their luck, and on this he maintained himself until a place was found for him, two years before his death, in Wellington's Ohiro rest home.

At the end of his life, McNish was filled with bitterness towards Shackleton—not for withholding the Polar Medal, nor for his general abandonment, but because Shackleton had killed his cat. People who knew him in his last years recall how he managed to work into every conversation the death of Mrs. Chippy. Alone, broken, with his heroism an abstract dream, Chippy McNish's thoughts turned to his one true mate, who he had boasted to a fellow seaman "had been such a special pet that she was known as Mrs. Chippy to the whole expedition."

McNish died in 1930, and for a pauper received an uncommon funeral. His pall-bearers were drawn from a Royal Navy ship, and the New Zealand Army supplied a gun carriage to carry his coffin. He was buried in an unmarked grave in Karori Cemetery, over which, in 1957, the New Zealand Antarctic Society erected a head-stone. McNish left only a single possession of any value—the diary he had kept on the *Endurance*.

Vincent became the skipper of a trawler, and died of pneumonia in his bunk on a date unknown. A single material record of his later life is known; an unexpectedly gracious letter that he wrote to Hudson's mother, assuring her that her son—whom he had last seen utterly incapacitated by exposure and frostbite on Elephant Island—was doing very well and had never failed to pull his weight. Holness also went back to the trawlers and was washed overboard in a storm. Stephenson died of cancer in a hospital in Hull.

Tom McLeod settled in Canada, fishing for two years off Bell's Island. He never married, claiming he "never had enough money to buy a house in which to put a wife." Unbeknownst to Shackleton, McLeod had secretly retrieved the Bible that the Boss had deposited on the ice after the breakup of the *Endurance*, believing it would be bad luck to leave it. He presented it to the family who looked after him in Punta Arenas, and they in turn presented it many years later to the Royal Geographical Society—where it remains, the pages torn from the Book of Job still missing. McLeod died at the age of eighty-seven, in a rest home in Canada.

Blackborow arrived back in Wales in late December, several months after his companions, and received a festive, enthusiastic welcome from his whole street. He volunteered for the navy, but was rejected on medical grounds, and so returned to sea until the end of the war, when he joined his father working at the Newport docks. He was often invited to speak about his experience, but was reluctant to do so and spoke instead of his companions. Although he wore a block shoe on his damaged foot, he never mentioned it, and had assiduously trained himself to walk without a limp. He stayed in touch with his old mates Bakewell and How; to this day, the descendents of these men have kept up correspondence. Blackborow died in 1949, at the age of fifty-four, of a heart condition and chronic bronchitis.

Bakewell stayed on in South America, sheep farming in Patagonia for a year; his subsequent occupations included merchant seaman, railroad switchman, and farmer. He settled in Dukes, Michigan, in 1945, where he worked as a dairy farmer and raised his daughter. In 1964, he was invited to England to attend the fiftieth anniversary of the departure of the expedition. His Michigan neighbors never knew of his adventures—since it was a British expedition, he figured they wouldn't be interested. He died at the age of eighty-one, in 1969.

After serving in the Royal Navy during the war, Rickinson became a naval architect and consulting engineer, and died in 1945. Kerr continued with the Merchant Service until his retirement. Hussey, whose heart, perhaps, had never been in his meteorological duties, became a medical doctor after serving in two world wars. During his lifetime he lectured frequently on the expedition. Although married he had no children, but before his death handed over his lecture notes and lantern slides to a young man he had chosen as his heir, with the injunction "to keep alive the story of the *Endurance*."

Marston collaborated with Hurley on a number of painted/photographic composites. In 1925, he joined an organization established to regenerate and support rural industries. He died in 1940, at the age of fifty-eight, of coronary thrombosis.

Hudson, after serving on mystery, or "Q," ships during the war, joined the British India Navigation Society. His health had been permanently impaired by the boat journey, frostbite having maimed his hands and caused necrosis of the bone of the lower back. At the time of his death he was a commodore of convoys in the Royal Naval Reserve, during the Second World War. He had returned from a Russian convoy when he was asked to take another mission to Gibraltar. He could have refused, but did not, and he was killed on his return trip.

After serving on a minesweeper during the war, Clark eventually took up an appointment at a fishery research station near Aberdeen, writing research papers on herring larvae and haddock investigations. He was locally renowned for his football and cricket prowess. He died in Aberdeen in 1950, at the age of sixty-eight.

In 1937, James immigrated to South Africa, where he took up the Chair of Physics at the University of Cape Town, eventually becoming vice-chancellor. During his tenure, he spoke out publically for the right to admit non-European students to the university. He died in 1964, aged seventy-three.

Wordie, later Sir James Wordie, became a highly distinguished geologist, president of the Royal Geographical Society, and the master of St. John's College, Cambridge. His expedition work in the Arctic received numerous awards, and he was responsible for inspiring a number of the next generation of polar explorers. He died in 1962, like his friend James at the age of seventy-three.

After serving as a medical officer in the war—for which he received a number of decorations, including the Military Cross—Macklin settled in Aberdeen. He eventually became head of Student Health Services at the University of Aberdeen, and remained in close contact with Clark. Macklin became one of the most important "historians" of both the *Endurance* expedition and Shackleton's later life. He died in

1967, aged seventy-seven. McIlroy joined the Orient Line after the war, and was aboard a vessel torpedoed in World War II. He endured a second open-boat journey before being rescued by the Vichy and taken to a camp in Sudan. He died in his eighties, a bachelor, but reportedly with girlfriends to the end.

Lees, while still in Punta Arenas, obtained a position in the Royal Flying Corps, with Shackleton's aid. Here, he took up the cause of acquiring parachutes for pilots, an innovation that was resisted by senior officers on the grounds that the possibility of bailing out would undermine a pilot's fighting spirit. To showcase parachutes' effectiveness, Lees parachuted off Tower Bridge, an event that was covered by the London newspapers. He later married a Japanese woman and settled in Japan and then New Zealand, working as a spy during the Second World War, an occupation eminently suited to his busybody, secretive nature. Lees may have been the most despised individual during the actual expedition, but it is impossible to dislike him posthumously. Without his busy, anxious chatter and compulsive candor, the record of the expedition would be much the poorer. Lees died at age seventy-nine in a mental hospital, the cause of death noted on his death certificate as "broncho-pneumonia—24 hours. Cardio-vascular degeneration. Senility?" Evidently, even the attending doctors could not quite get a handle on him. He was buried in the ex-servicemen's section of the Karori Cemetery—the same little patch of earth in which McNish was laid. The two men had loathed each other.

After the *Quest* expedition, Frank Wild settled in South Africa, where four years of drought and floods ruined his cotton farming. Drink, however, was the ultimate cause of his ruination; his ominous zeal in adopting the "Gut Rot" toasts on Elephant Island had always been a source of amusement to his companions. A newspaper journalist discovered Wild working as a bartender for £4 a month in a Zulu village at the head of a mine. "Teddy" Evans, whose life Crean had saved on Scott's last expedition, hearing word of the plight of a man whom he regarded as a shipmate and great polar explorer, assisted him in obtaining a pension; but the boon came too late, and Wild died only months afterward, in 1939.

Tom Crean returned to Anascaul, where he had been born; he married, opened a pub called the South Pole Inn, and raised a family.

"We had a hot time of it the last 12 months," wrote Crean to an old shipmate from the *Terra Nova*, succinctly summarizing the months on the floes, the two boat journeys, and the crossing of South Georgia. "And I must say the Boss is a splendid gentleman and I done my duty towards him to the end."

He led an organized, disciplined life, working in the pub and in his garden, and each evening taking a walk down to the sea in Dingle Bay with his dogs Fido and Toby, named after the pups he had lost in the Antarctic. He was said by those who knew him to have admired Scott but loved Shackleton. He died of a perforated appendix in 1938, and was buried just outside Anascaul.

Worsley spent the greater part of his life trying to recapture the thrill and daring of the *Endurance* expedition. During the war, while captain of a mystery ship, he sank a German submarine, for which he received a Distinguished Service Order. He then joined Shackleton in Russia, and stayed on after the war fighting the Bolsheviks, which won him a second Distinguished Service Order. After the *Quest*, he was co-leader of an Arctic expedition, and appears to have spent a fair amount of time attempting to re-create the experience aboard the *Endurance* by almost deliberately getting stuck in the ice. In 1934, he went treasure hunting in the Pacific, something he and Shackleton had promised each other they would do together. In the Second World War, he was given command of a merchant ship but was sacked when it was discovered that he was nearly seventy years old. He died of lung cancer in 1943, just short of seventy-one.

His duties to the expedition completed, Hurley was appointed official photographer and awarded the honorary rank of captain with the Australian Imperial Force. Within days of signing up he was covering the struggle at Ypres. His photographs clearly show that he got close to the action, and some are small masterpieces of stark, muddy misery. His Paget slides from this period are some of the very few known color images of the First World War. A distinction was made by his superiors between historical and propaganda shots, and Hurley chose to furnish the latter. It was during this period that his passion for composites became excessive; glorious, mournful skyscapes, exploding shells, puffs of ominous smoke, clouds of primitive planes like dragonflies—all are liberally imposed upon his original images.

After the war, he continued his demanding pace, making photographic expeditions to Papua New Guinea and Tasmania, and in the Second World War he was sent to Palestine. He married a beautiful young Spanish-French opera singer ten days after meeting her, and they had three children, to whom he was a loving but stern father. Following the Second World War, he created a great number of photographic books intended to promote the various regions of Australia. He travelled indefatigably to produce these, and all are competent; but it is difficult, indeed, to reconcile the perky, picture-postcard images with the bold, elegant, and at times emotionally momentous photographs of the *Endurance* expedition. At the end of his life, he produced several books on Australian and Tasmanian wildflowers.

At the age of seventy-six, still on assignment, still lugging his heavy camera gear, Hurley came home from a day's work and mentioned to his wife that he felt ill. So unusual was it for him to make such a complaint that the family was instantly put on alert. Wrapping himself in his dressing gown, he took to his favorite chair and refused to budge. A doctor was summoned, but Hurley curtly motioned him away. He was still sitting in his chair the following morning, grimly, tenaciously, and silently waging his war with imminent death. Around noon of the same day, January 16, 1962, he finally passed away.

In 1970, the three surviving members of the expedition were invited to attend the ceremony for the commissioning of the HMS *Endurance*. A photograph shows them, three elderly men, sitting in folding chairs, under the Union Jack.

Walter How, able seaman on the *Endurance*, returned to his home in London, after service in the Merchant Navy. He had intended to join the *Quest*, but at the last moment chose to remain with his father, who had become ill. Although his sight was failing, owing in part to a land-mine accident during the war, How became an amateur painter and builder of ships in bottles; his detailed models and sketches of the *Endurance* betray that her lines were etched upon his memory. He was also one of the most loyal alumni of the expedition, going to great lengths to try to stay in touch with all hands. He died at the age of eighty-seven, in 1972.

Green, the cook, had written a letter to his parents when he signed on with Shackleton in Buenos Aires in 1914, but the ship carrying his message was torpedoed, so that no one knew where he was. On return to civilization in 1916, he, like others of the crew, had to find his own way home—officers and scientists returned on a liner—and eventually got a passage as a "distressed British seaman." Back in England, he discovered that his parents had cashed in his life insurance policy and that his girlfriend had married. He moved to Hull to be with his mates, the unsympathetic trawlerhands. After the war, he continued his career as a ship's cook, and also gave lantern slide lectures on the expedition. Excerpts from an interview suggest that these lectures may have contained erroneous, eccentric details (all food lost when the *Endurance* was tilted on her side! dogs disembarked to lighten the ship!). During a tour of duty in New Zealand, he gave his lecture in Wellington, where he met McNish, who had been let out of hospital for the occasion. When Green saw McNish in the audience, he invited him up to the stand, where the carpenter took the lecture over and "gave the boat journey." Green died in 1974, at the age of eighty-six, of peritonitis.

Lionel Greenstreet's war service had begun in Buenos

Greenstreet illustrating breath icicles

"Some of his jokes & stories are decidedly humourous & after all one cannot exactly expect to keep up drawing-room standard in a mixed assembly such as ours." (Lees, diary)

Aires, when he took command of a tug returning to Britain. During the Second World War, he served on rescue tugs in the Atlantic. He retired to Devon, although he still kept up his London Club. He retained his somewhat breezy, caustic sense of humor to the end. He was mistakenly reported as dead in 1964, and took great pleasure in informing the newspapers that his obituary was premature. He died in March 1979, at the age of eighty-nine, having been the last of the *Endurance* survivors. While it is not difficult to conjure up the long-past events of the expedition, it bankrupts the imagination to try to conceive that a man who sailed with Shackleton in the barquentine *Endurance* would live to see others walk upon the moon.

In Hurley's photographic record of the *Endurance*, perhaps the single most memorable and representative image depicts a line of ragged men standing on the beach of Elephant Island, wildly cheering as the lifeboat from the *Yelcho* heaves into view; Hurley called it "The Rescue." When published by Worsley in his memoir, *Endurance*, however, this same scene is entitled "The Departure of the *James Caird* from Elephant Island." The original film negative, in the archives of the Royal Geographical Society, shows that the *Caird* has been violently scratched out, leaving the supply boat—the *Stancomb Wills*—and her waving crew as they make their way back to land. The explanation for Hurley's action is simple: An appropriately climactic photographic ending to the story was needed for the lectures.

Hurley's predilection for "fiddling" with his images was usually harmless, but in this case, he committed a grave indiscretion, for the original, irretrievable image was the greater. In it, he captured both sides of this impossible story, the razor's edge of its endeavor—success and failure in the balance, the momentous departure and the patient bravery of those left behind to wait, their hands raised boldly in a determined, resigned, and courageous farewell.

"The Departure of the James Caird *from Elephant Island."*

Haircutting tournament

"No dogs out today as it is to dark crew ice ship we all had our hair cut to the scalp & then had our photograph taken after in the Ritz we do look a lot of convicts & we are not much short of that life at present." (McNish, diary)

Acknowledgments

The number of institutions and individuals who have helped me on this book is very great. I would first like to acknowledge the American Museum of Natural History for their collaboration on both this book and the exhibition that it accompanies. The exhibition, *Endurance: Shackleton's Legendary Expedition*, will display virtually all the Frank Hurley photographs to survive the expedition, as well as all known surviving objects—including, courtesy of Dulwich College, the *James Caird*. The exhibition was made possible by a major gift from Mr. and Mrs. Joseph F. Cullman III. For this and for their enthusiasm and interest, I am more grateful than I can say.

Grateful thanks are also due to Ellen V. Futter, the museum's president, and Anne Sidaman-Eristoff, its chairman, for their support of the exhibition. I would like to give particular thanks to Dr. Craig Morris, dean of science, and Maron L. Waxman, associate director for special publishing, as well as to my colleagues David Harvey, director of exhibitions, Joel Sweimler, exhibition coordinator, Ross MacPhee, curator of mammalogy, and Cynthia Woodward, for their hard work and enthusiasm. My good friend Jenny Lawrence, editor at *Natural History*, acted as adviser and sounding board at early stages of both the book and the exhibition. Rose Wadsworth, coordinator of travelling exhibits, provided early guidance as well. Also to be thanked are Maria Yakimov, registrar, and Pat Dandonoli, executive director for institutional planning and media production, and designer Paul De Pass, who worked with the Exhibition Department.

The majority of the photographs were printed courtesy of the Royal Geographical Society, London, directly from Frank Hurley's surviving glass plate and film negatives. Since its foundation in 1830, the Royal Geographical Society has organized and financed numerous expeditions of discovery, and was indeed a contributor to Shack-

Acknowledgments

leton's 1914–16 expedition on the *Endurance.* The society's photographic holdings are priceless and legendary, and yet among even these the Hurley collection holds a certain pride of place. Much gratitude is owed to Dr. Rita Gardner, the society's president, as well as to Nigel de N. Winser, deputy director of the society; the latter was receptive and encouraging when the exhibition was merely a figment of my imagination. Particular thanks are owed to Joanna Scadden, picture library manager, for overseeing the complicated photographic printing process. Dr. A. F. Tatham, keeper of the society's archives, was helpful in providing documents and various items—including the Bible Shackleton thought he had left behind on the ice!

Scott Polar Research Institute, University of Cambridge, provided the second part of the Hurley collection, allowing prints to be made from their album of unique and less well known Hurley photographs. I am grateful to the institute's helpful staff and would like to thank in particular Dr. Robert Headland, archivist and curator of the institute's remarkable collection of documents, photographs, and manuscripts. In the course of my visits to the institute, Dr. Headland steered me through the many diaries and other papers, and was always unstinting in his advice and comments. I am also particularly grateful to Philippa Smith, picture library manager, for her cheerful and efficient help in obtaining prints and odds and ends of research. The diaries of Sir Ernest Shackleton, Reginald James, Lionel Greenstreet (on microfilm), Thomas Orde-Lees, and Frank Worsley were read at Scott Polar Research Institute, as were the correspondence of many of these men, the papers of Shackleton's biographers Margery and James Fisher, and Lees's unpublished memoir, "Beset by Berg and Floe." I also read here Worsley's typescript memoirs of the two boat journeys and the crossing of South Georgia. All quotations from these works are made with the kind permission of the institute.

The prints appearing in both this book and the exhibition were all produced by Barbara and Michael Gray, of Fox Talbot Museum. I am very grateful to them for both their superb work and for the information they supplied me about Hurley's photographic methods.

The Mitchell Library, State Library of New South Wales, Sydney, Australia, furnished microfilms of Frank Hurley's diary and Frank Wild's *Memoirs*, the originals of which are in their collection. It is also from their collection that Hurley's photograph of John Vincent (originally in Paget color) is reproduced. I am also extremely grateful to Tim Lovell-Smith of the Alexander Turnbull Library in Wellington, New Zealand, for the loan of microfilm copies of the diaries of Frank Worsley (made courtesy of Scott Polar Research Institute), Henry McNish, and Thomas Orde-Lees, the originals of which are in their collection. One volume of Orde-Lees diary is in the possession of Dartmouth College Special Collections. Quotations from the diaries cited were made with the kind permission of these libraries.

Above all, I am grateful to the families of the expedition members and a number of independent scholars. No project I have ever worked on has elicited such generous and unconditional offers of assistance. Diaries and documents that had been safeguarded for many years were made available to me with no strings attached. Others shared the fruits of many years' private labor, or the contents of unpublished works in progress; not one individual ever asked for so much as a printed credit. Without the information and source material provided by these families and scholars it would not have been possible to write this book.

Alexandra Shackleton, the granddaughter of the great explorer, was very generous with her time and family possessions, as well as very entertaining to be with.

Peter Wordie and Mrs. Alison Stancer provided me with a hitherto unseen copy of their father's diary, a fascinating and very precise document that I drew on heavily. They were also extremely forthcoming with other papers and items of interest.

Mrs. Elizabeth Rajala made available the unpublished autobiography of her father, William Bakewell, along with other papers and photographs.

The entire Blackborow family—son, grandson, and great-granddaughter, as well as, incredibly, sister and brother, of Shackleton's stowaway—gave me a warm welcome and provided much information about Perce Blackborow.

Thomas McNeish not only provided information and records about his grandfather, but was also, with his wife, Jessie, a hospitable host of a very enjoyable visit to their home. Isabel and Donald Laws, and Iris Johnstone from other branches of McNeish's family, became indefatigable sleuths of that highly interesting if mysterious subject, "Chippy" McNeish.

Dr. Richard Hudson graciously received me at his home to see the sextant his father had loaned to Worsley for navigating the *Caird*, and also let me peruse the numerous papers his father had left.

The Macklin family was generous in their offer to let me use the diary of their father, as well as his voluminous correspondence and related papers. I was also fortunate to have discussed certain members of the crew with the late Jean Macklin, Dr. Alexander Macklin's wife.

Mrs. Doris Warren kindly sent me copies of papers and photographs pertaining to her father, Walter How.

Mrs. Toni Mooy-Hurley and Adélie Hurley were generous with vivid reminiscences about their father, Frank Hurley, and for their permission to quote from his diaries and use his photographs.

Acknowledgments

Julian Ayer very kindly allowed me access to his grandfather Thomas Orde-Lees's photographic negatives, and filled me in on aspects of his grandfather's history.

I am very grateful to Father Gerard O'Brien for information about his grandfather Tom Crean, and to Crean's godson, John Knightly, for information about the great explorer. The Kerry County Council kindly provided me with copies of documents pertaining to Crean.

Richard Greenstreet gave me biographical material pertaining to his uncle: The quotations from Lionel Greenstreet's diary and correspondence are made with his kind permission.

Roy Cockram provided me with wonderful biographical and anecdotal material about Charles Green, his uncle.

I am grateful to Roland Huntford, both for information and advice given in person at a very early stage of my "discovery" of Shackleton, and for his magisterial works on Scott, Amundsen, and Shackleton. Two other distinguished Antarctic historians, Ann Shirley and Margaret Slythe, were very helpful in directing me to people and sources.

I am more grateful than I can say to Margot Morrell for the generous gift of her transcripts of the diaries of Hurley and Orde-Lees. Shane Murphy shared the fruits of his many years' close study of Hurley's *Endurance* collection, which is to be published under the title *According to Hoyle*.

Maureen Mahood shared with me her careful work on the men who remained on Elephant Island, to be published in a work entitled *Counting the Days*. The documents, photographs, and many references she generously forwarded to me proved invaluable.

Leif Mills provided me with much biographical material about Frank Wild, which will be published in a forthcoming book entitled *Wild*. John Bell Thomson, author of *Shackleton's Captain: A Biography of Frank Worsley* (Hazard Press, 1998), gave me a wealth of material about Worsley; his recent book is the only comprehensive account of the legendary navigator.

I am grateful to Geoffrey Selley and Ralph Gullett for information about Leonard Hussey—and for the stanzas from Hussey's facetious poem.

Mary DeLashmit, of the Holderness Free Library, supplied me with countless books and microfilms through interlibrary loan services; I do not know how I would have managed without her efficient help.

Harding Dunnett, chairman of the *James Caird* Society, Dulwich, England, was my guiding angel. His encyclopedic and precise memory saved me weeks of time on many occasions. I am especially grateful for my visit with him to see the *Caird*, on display at Dulwich College, which was a deeply moving experience.

Robert Burton, keeper of the South Georgia Island Whaling Museum, was forthcoming with documents, photographs, and information, and has been a very helpful ally. James Meiklejohn, secretary of the Salvesen Ex-Whalers Club, in Norway, supplied me with fascinating material from the Norwegian whalers on South Georgia. Thomas Binnie Jr. also supplied me with material from the South Georgia side. Dan Weinstein was a kind of guru to me when I first embarked upon this subject, guiding me to many knowledgeable sources.

I am very grateful to Baden Norris of the Canterbury Museum, Christchurch, for his information on "Chippy" McNish's last years. Two articles were very helpful to me: Judith Lee Hallock's "Thomas Crean," in *Polar Record* 22, no. 140 (1985): 665–78; and Stephen Locke's "George Marston," in *Polar Record* 33, no. 184 (1997): 65–70.

I would also like to thank George Butler, Isobel Crombie, Philip Cronenwett, Jenny Gioponlos, Richard Kossaw, Ivo Meisner, Gael Newton, Laura Bemis Rollison, Jeff Rubin, Sarah Scully, Peter Speak and Robert Stephenson. My thanks also to Dorothy Cullman for her early encouragement.

As always, I am grateful to my friend and agent, Anthony Sheil, for guiding this complex project.

Thanks are due to George Andreou, my editor, and to Peter Andersen and Andy Hughes, the book's long-suffering designer and production director, respectively, at Knopf.

A number of published books offer opportunities to explore the story of this expedition further. Roland Huntford's *Shackleton* (reissued in 1998 by Atheneum) is the comprehensive biography of Shackleton's life, and was my primary source for the years between the *Endurance* and *Quest* expeditions. Huntford's previous work, *Scott and Amundsen* (Atheneum, rev. ed. 1983), which provides vivid background to Shackleton's undertaking, is a landmark work; it pulls no punches from Scott, for which it has been both widely praised and criticized, depending upon which side of the Scott/Shackleton camp one champions—feelings about both men still run very high! Personally tending towards Huntford's view, I found this work both mesmerizing and invaluable. *Shackleton*, by Margery and James Fisher (James Barrie Books, 1957), was written when many of the expedition members were still alive to be interviewed.

Shackleton's own account of his adventure, *South* (Heinemann, 1919), is, of course, a classic. Also not to be missed are Frank Worsley's two books, *Endurance* (Philip Allen, 1931) and *Shackleton's Boat Journey* (recently reissued by W. W. Norton). Less

Acknowledgments

well known are Captain Frank Hurley's two books, *Argonauts of the South* (G. P. Putnam's Sons, 1925) and *Shackleton's Argonauts* (Angus and Robertson, 1948). Leonard Hussey's *South With Shackleton* (Sampson Low, 1949) is also rewarding. *Shackleton's Last Voyage: The Story of the Quest*, by Frank Wild (Cassell and Company, 1923), is the story of the last voyage.

Alfred Lansing's *Endurance: Shackleton's Incredible Voyage* (Carroll & Graf, 1986, and illus. hardcover ed., The Adventure Library, 1994) and is a rip-roaring narration of the *Endurance* epic. Harding Dunnett's recent *Shackleton's Boat: The Story of the James Caird* (Neville & Harding, 1996) is a fascinating A-to-Z of the legendary boat. Two valuable books tell the tragic and heroic story of the less well known half of the expedition: *The Ross Sea Shore Party, 1914–1917*, by R. W. Richards (Scott Polar Research Institute, 1962); and *Shackleton's Forgotten Argonauts*, by Lennard Bickel (Macmillan, 1982).

A number of books have been published, all in Australia, about Frank Hurley and his work: *In Search of Frank Hurley*, by Lennard Bickel (Macmillan 1980), and *Once More on My Adventure*, by Frank Legg and Toni Hurley (Ure Smith, 1966). *Hurley at War: The Photography and Diaries of Frank Hurley in Two World Wars* (Fairfax Library in association with Daniel O'Keefe, 1986) includes examples of Hurley's rare color images from the First World War. *Frank Hurley in Papua: Photographs of the 1920–1923 Expeditions*, by Jim Specht and John Fields (Robert Brown and Associates, 1984), presents what is probably Hurley's best work next to the *Endurance* photographs.

A NOTE ON THE PHOTOGRAPHS

An article published in the *Australasian Photo-Review* of August 22, 1914, shortly before Hurley's departure on the *Endurance* expedition, describes his choice of photographic equipment:

> The leader of the Expedition left the choice of photographic apparatus and outfit for the entire trip entirely to Mr. Hurley, and it shows to what perfection the local supplies have been brought when the Sydney branch of Kodak (Australasia) Ltd. was able to supply from stock everything required. . . .
>
> Included in the items were Graflex cameras and a square bellows stand plate camera for use where weight was unimportant. For the sledging parties entire reliance is placed on various sized Kodaks, including V.P.K. [Vest Pocket Kodak], No. 3 and 3A F.P.K. and of course, for use in the latter, an ample supply of the ever dependable Kodak N.C. film. For the plate cameras a large supply of Austral Standard plates (backed) is available, and also Austral lantern plates, so that slides may be made on the spot. Most of the cameras are fitted with Cooke lenses of varying foci and apertures, including the well-known 12 inch f/3.5 Portrait lens. For some special work a 17 inch Ross f/5.4 Telecentric finds a place.

When the *Endurance* sank, Hurley managed to save whole (6¾" x 8½") and half (4¾" x 6½") plate glass negatives; these are now in the possession of the Royal Geographical Society's Picture Library. He also salvaged an album of photographs he had already printed; these album photographs represent mostly informal portraits of life on board ship before disaster struck. This album is in the archives of Scott Polar Research Institute, Cambridge University. Twenty surviving Paget color transparencies, extremely rare examples of early color photography, are in the possession of the Mitchell Library, State Library of New South Wales, Australia. Finally, Hurley took thirty-eight photographs with his small hand-held Vest Pocket Kodak after he was forced to abandon his equipment at Ocean Camp; these film images are also in the collection of the Royal Geographical Society.

The photographs in this book were all made from the original glass plate and film negatives, or from interpositives made directly from the album photographs. The duotone reproductions were matched as closely as possible to prints that Hurley made of his own negatives shortly after the *Endurance* expedition. Boldface captions accompanying most photographs are Hurley's own captions for those images.

The American Museum of Natural History's exhibition *Endurance: Shackleton's Legendary Expedition* represents the most comprehensive exhibition of Frank Hurley's work from the *Endurance* expedition ever mounted. All of the photographic prints, both for the exhibition and for this book, were produced by Barbara and Michael Gray at their studio near Bath. Michael Gray is the curator of the National Trust, Fox Talbot Museum, Lacock, England.

Hurley filming from the mast

"Hurley is a warrior with his camera & would go anywhere or do anything to get a picture."
(*Greenstreet, letter to his father*)

A NOTE ABOUT THE AUTHOR

Caroline Alexander, who has written for *The New Yorker*, *Granta*, *Smithsonian*, *Outside*, and *National Geographic*, among other publications, is the author of four previous books. She is the curator of *Endurance: Shackleton's Legendary Expedition*, an exhibition that will open at the American Museum of Natural History in March 1999. She lives on a farm in New Hampshire.

A NOTE ON THE TYPE

The text of this book was set in Van Dijck, a modern revival of a typeface attributed to the Dutch master punchcutter Christoffel van Dyck, c. 1606–1669. The revival was produced by the Monotype Corporation in 1937–1938 with the assistance, and perhaps over the objection, of the Dutch typographer Jan van Krimpen. Never in wide use, Monotype Van Dijck nonetheless has the familiar and comfortable qualities of the types of William Caslon, who used the original Van Dijck as the model for his famous type.

Composed by Stratford Publishing Services, Brattleboro, Vermont
Halftones prepared by Barbara and Michael Gray
Printed and bound by Butler & Tanner, Frome, England

Designed by Peter A. Andersen